FATHER'S DAY

Jason S. Glenn
Ronald L. Glenn

Sigfam Media Group, LLC

P.O. Box 27
Wilberforce, Ohio 45384
http://www.sigfam.com

Cover and graphic designs by Rev. Samuel A. Harris, Jr.

Acknowledgments

The authors are especially grateful to Sandra Samson, Jessie Alexander, L. Michelle Odom, Paul Gates, and Janie S. Glenn for critical readings of early drafts of this book, and to Rev. Samuel A. Harris, Jr. for graphic designs, layout and other significant technical assistance.

Dedication

This book is dedicated to fathers of all types: expectant fathers, surrogate fathers, stepfathers, foster fathers, stay-at-home fathers, biological fathers, grandfathers, divorced fathers, future fathers, and even the deadbeat fathers who were rolling stones.

Why We Write

Father and son need to talk sometimes
Even when the words don't rhyme
And thoughts go on in new directions
Skirting round the tension sections
Because now and then I hear you say
You hear me in a brand new way
So it makes me think and be reflective
As I listen from a new perspective
To this compilation of verse
Welcome [son, dad] to my universe

Psalm 45:1-2

My heart is stirred by a noble theme
as I recite my verses for the king;
my tongue is the pen of a skillful writer.
You are the most excellent of men
and your lips have been anointed with grace,
since God has blessed you forever.

Contents

It's all in the family

Father's Day 3
A Funny Thing Happened While I Was Washing My Car . . 6
Grandpa's Second Chance 11
Family Business 13

Direction→home

A Reflection 15
Drive Time Epiphanies 16
Blind Spot 20

I ain't your...

That Word 23
From Mother to Son 26
What's in a Name? 27
A Father's Sacrifice 30

All that looks dumb, ain't

Hip Hop is Not Dead 35
Stolen Minds 41

Roots

Where You From? 44
H.N.I.C. 48
In the Woodpile 50
The Remedy 51

Look at our world, people

The Snitch 54
Playground 56
Who's Next? 59
Traveling Mercies 60

An awesome God

Flirting with the Master 68
The Father Who Wanted More 72
After Thanksgiving 76

Church folk

Singing on the Choir 82
The Janitor 85
Rock Star Status 90
Songbirds 94

Chance encounters

Humbug 97
The Run-in 99

Stuff happens

The Proposition 103
Stink 105

Swimming in the fountain of youth

Made Right 108
The Step Show 110
Man Enough 113
The Old Man Speaks 114

Healing time

Evolution 117

We Don't Give Out Pens: Lazy, Hazy, Crazy 120

PSA 128

What Kind of Love is This? 130

Fatherhood

Wailing 136

Out of Step 139

Who Are You? 141

Why? 145

Epilogue

Who Are These Boys? 147

Preface

The Reverend Edward Cross tells the story of a life-changing conversation with his grandmother when he was about thirteen years old. She and his parents had taught him to value education greatly. So he asked her one day, "Mema, tell me about your school." She refused and said that it was not important to talk about such things. He persistently tried for several days in a row to get her to respond. Finally, one day she relented and said, "I only went to school one day." He was stunned. "Only one day?" he muttered. "Yes," she replied, "I only went to school one day, but I stayed all day."

Sometimes life only gives us one day. If we stay all day, we will learn the lesson. This collection of essays, poems and homilies is about men who learned the lesson of the day.

It's all in the family

Father's Day

A Funny Thing Happened While I Was

Washing My Car

Grandpa's Second Chance

Family Business

1. Father's Day

It's Father's Day
I should be glad
It's Father's Day
Why do I feel
So sad?
The Temps sang it
And we went along
Even laughed about
The errant one
Whose name I should have
If he had not denied
What DNA now proves
In the blinking eye
He got that nut
Like the slickest squirrel
But ran off and
Left that girl
With me
To hang on her breast
To feed my hunger
And thirst
Lest I cry or whine
Or worst die
For the touch
Of the rolling stone
Who should be
Gathering moss
Near my home
And telling the world
I am his own
It's Father's Day

Let's celebrate
My paternal potentate
Despite the impulse to hate
Him for slip sliding away
When we begged him to stay
He chose to put us on the shelf
And left to be by himself
Somewhere else
Alone not with me
Late at night
As Father's Day
Slips away
I think I might learn to say
"Dad, I love you anyway"
It's irrational
It makes no sense
Passing time has placed a fence
Of separation between
And moved you
From the movie screen
Of my mind.
How can I even show affection
When your dutiful dereliction
Screams your absentee ballot
Was not cast for me
How can I love you
When I don't know you?
I can't even hug you
Or show you
How I feel
Even now I bow and kneel
Before the human
Who rules in me
Through the genetic sea

That decrees
My eyes my nose
My slew-foot stance
Anyone can see at a glance
I am his and he is mine
He and mom at least, one time
Commingled essence fluidly
To produce the one
Who became me
It's Father's Day
I should be sad
It's Father's Day
Why do I feel so glad?

rlg

2. A Funny Thing Happened While I Was Washing My Car

I got up early one Saturday morning and decided to go wash my car. The day at that point was nothing out of the ordinary, just a regular Saturday. The sun was shining. The birds were chirping. Everything was as good as it could be for a guy in my situation.

I had just finished scrubbing my tires, when I noticed this church group walking through my apartment complex. They were all dressed in matching T-shirts and holding those little cans with the slits in the top that people usually carry when they are going around asking for money. It turns out that they were collecting donations for the youth group at their church. One of the ladies in the group, who looked about my age, maybe a few years older, walked up to me and asked for a donation. I didn't have much cash on me, but I had just finished cleaning out the interior of my car. I had some spare change in my pocket that I had found underneath one of my seats. I plopped a couple of quarters down in her can and went back to washing my car.

However, the lady said that the purpose of the group's excursion was not only to collect donations, but to testify and spread the Word. Therefore, she began to talk to me about Jesus and his love. At some point she asked me if I knew Jesus. I exclaimed that my father is a preacher and has been all of my life, so Jesus and I have met--even though I don't keep in touch with him as often as I should. She apparently saw this as her opportunity to help me get back in touch with Jesus, and invited me to her church on Sunday. It seemed like a reasonable proposition at the time, so I told her I would think about it. She then became thrilled at the idea that she had possibly just saved another heathen, and continued the conversation with much zeal. She told me a little bit about herself. She was recently divorced, she had two kids, and she just started a new job that she was really excited about. Then she began to ask about me. I told her that I was in school and that I have a baby daughter.

"A baby girl?" she exclaimed. "How precious! Do you have any pictures?"

Although I did have a picture of her in my wallet, I lied and said no. I'm not sure why, but I just didn't feel comfortable showing my daughter's picture to a complete stranger. There probably was no harm in doing so, but I decided to play it safe.

"What's her name?" she asked.

"Dallas," I replied.

Then a funny thing happened. At the mere mention of my daughter's name, the lady immediately cocked her head back and frowned up her face as if someone had just forced her to suck on a peeled lemon.

"Why you name that baby a man's name?" she spewed. I have to admit, the question caught me off guard. Granted, Dallas Glenn, my daughter's namesake, was a man. He was my great-grandfather. That is one of the main reasons why the name Dallas has meaning for me. Naming my daughter Dallas gives her a link to her history. Every time someone calls her name, they are invoking the spirit of one of her paternal ancestors. I hope that it will, in turn, act as a reminder that she will always be blanketed with the love and protection of not only her father, but also her grandfather and her great-grandfather and her great-great-grandfather, and the list goes on. One of the things that I also liked about my daughter's name is that it is versatile--gender neutral. I have, contrary to popular belief, actually come across several women named Dallas. It's a name that can be masculine when referring to a male, and feminine when referring to a female.

Nevertheless, I feel like in either case, it has strength and character, and I like that.

I didn't really feel the need to defend my decision to name my daughter Dallas, especially to some stranger, but I thought I could possibly enlighten the lady. Consequently, I took the time to explain the meaning behind my daughter's name. In spite of the fact that I didn't owe her any explanation in the first place, the lady was obviously not satisfied with the one I gave. She told me that her pastor had just preached a sermon on this topic. She began to quote some obscure scripture passage--something that included the phrase, "...and the children shall be named...," or something like that. Then she said, "You have to take something like naming a child seriously. You don't know. Naming that child a man's name might make her grow up to be a lesbian or something."
In a surprisingly calm tone, I explained my theory that lesbianism had less to do with one's name, and more to do with one's desire to sleep with women. Unfortunately, my hypothesis fell on deaf ears. I then became really annoyed, to say the least.

Now, normally, if I find myself in a situation where I think someone is talking complete nonsense, then I will just walk away. I don't normally lash out at the offender or engage in confrontation, but in this case I was at my house, minding my own business and this lady came and forced her unsolicited, unwanted opinion on me. Therefore, I didn't think I should be the one to leave. Plus, I hadn't yet rinsed my car. I felt backed into a corner, and if I followed my normal modus operandi, it would mean interrupting what I was doing. In addition, I think fathers, especially fathers of little girls, have an inherent instinct to want to protect their children from would-be threats, even if the threat happens to be the benign, nonsensical, ramblings of a stranger. I would like to tell you that I summoned the infinite wisdom passed down to me from my father and his father and his father before him. I would like to say that I then used that wisdom to say something profound, poignant, and meaningful; but, alas, I was left to my own devices. I turned to the lady, and interjected in the middle of her Jesus tirade, something that I have to admit could be viewed as a bit mean-spirited. I said, "You know, Roushedra, you may have a point. Maybe I should be concerned about the affect that my daughter's name will have on her in the future because it's obvious that your name must be what turned you ugly."

For some reason, she didn't seem at all pleased with the fact that I had taken her words of wisdom into account. In fact, she promptly popped open her can, gave me my quarters back, quoted some more Bible verses, told me I needed Jesus, and stormed off. Initially, I found it ironic that the conflict between this lady and me started because she insulted me; yet, in the end, she decided that I was the one who needed Jesus. Now that I think about it, maybe she was right. I think that God has a sense of humor. So maybe, in His own comical way, God was trying to show me that I do need Jesus.

Once again, I have to admit that Jesus and I don't always talk as much as maybe we should. I, like so many others, am wrestling with questions of faith, and I'm far from the end of my spiritual journey. However, I do believe in the lessons that Jesus taught--the universal lessons of love and respect and caring for others--the lessons that I learned from my father that were passed down from his father, and his father before him, and so on.

I'm sure that there probably was a better way to respond to the lady's comments that morning. I still have many lessons to learn, lessons that I may one day be able to give to my daughter from my own bank of fatherly wisdom. I'm sure that there will once again come a time when I will feel the need to spring to my daughter's defense; and just maybe, Jesus willing, with the help of my paternal ancestors, when that time comes, I'll be able to say something profound, poignant and meaningful.

jsg

3. Grandpa's Second Chance

I'm Grandpa now
I've learned my lessons
From all of life's
Classroom sessions
I really messed up
The first time around
With my sons and daughters
Who think I'm a clown
I'm glad God is good
All the time
So terrible starts
Work out just fine
God gave me
Another chance
The time to see
If I could advance
My parenting skills
To the grand fatherly level
A chance to fulfill
The need that bedevils
But she won't come to me
She runs just as fast
As her chubby legs
Will take her right past
Grandpa's outstretched arms
Reaching out with love
Trying in vain to charm
This skipping ladybug
They say it's my beard
I refuse to cut it off
I would shave it back

But I have to count the cost
She won't cut me any slack
Though she doesn't run as fast
As she used to
When she saunters past
Maybe a threat will help
"Out of my will you go!"
She is only two years old
She doesn't seem worried, so
Maybe a bribe will work
Perhaps a special treat
I feel like such a jerk
As the scene repeats
She doesn't even stop
To give me another glance
Doesn't she know
This is grandpa's last chance?

rlg

4. Family Business

What's that to you?
Daddy asked
Outside children named at last
Family secrets hidden within
Outsiders knew about all the sins
My sister, my brother
Way cross town
The rumors were true
That they spread around
The Stone stopped rolling
Now and then
Producing unknown
Next of kin
That's family business
You're talking about
There's no need
For you to doubt
Intrusion of lust erstwhile
Did produce an outside child
Daddy's home now
Settled down
Faithful to his
Marriage vow
Respect him, love him
If he stays
Curse him, damn him
If he strays
He won't go far
This time around
Age and infirmities
Have slowed him down.

rlg

Direction→home

A Reflection

Drive Time Epiphanies

Blind Spot

5. A Reflection

A reflection on steel town roots
Early morning snow clings to a pair of
Slightly scuffed, barely broken-in boots
As I climb this hill that seems to go on forever.
This
A journey I've made many times before
But never in this condition

Just moments earlier I felt no pain
But as I feel blood trickling down my nose it sets in
Panic!

Move faster!
Get home now!
One fateful step onto unseen ice
And here I am
I turn the corner and see this house of red brick
So familiar.
The door opens
And there stands
A man
Who is larger than life
With a look of sincere concern

By the end of the day
I have
Six stitches
A chipped tooth
A band-aid
And an appreciation for a man
With my last name.

jsg

6. Drive Time Epiphanies

I like to drive. Some people really hate the idea of sitting in traffic or dealing with tailgaters and road rage--but not me. I actually love driving. This affinity serves me well because it takes me at least twenty minutes to get to school and work when there is no traffic. I am usually in my car during a significant portion of most days, but I enjoy more than just the physical driving experience, because I also love to think. Since driving gives me uninterrupted alone time, I do some of my best thinking when I'm in my car.

Sometimes while I'm driving and thinking, I'll begin to reflect on different events in my life, analyze my choices and actions in those situations, and think about the alternative choices or actions that I could have made. Inevitably, during these moments of reflection, I will have an epiphany, at which point I can't help but exclaim aloud, "I'll be darned if the old man wasn't right!"

You see, when I was a teenager, I thought, as most teenagers do, that I knew everything there was to know about everything. No one could tell me otherwise. Furthermore, I concluded that anyone who tried to convince me that I still had more to learn about the world, didn't know nothin' about nothin'. This rule was especially true if the person trying to tell me something, happened to be one of my parents. There is a subtle irony in the fact that I now have these moments of clarity while I'm driving because my father, a man who was later proven to actually know somethin', is the person who taught me how to drive.

I can vividly remember sitting in the driver's seat of gold Honda Civic early one Saturday morning when I was sixteen. My father sat in the passenger seat and appeared eerily calm for a man who was about to risk his life at the hands of his very inexperienced son. He could tell that I was chomping at the bit, so he began with his characteristically cool and steady voice to give me directions.

"Adjust your seat ."

"O.K. Now, check your mirrors ."

"Just get used to the feel of the driver's seat. Learn to appreciate the privilege of driving ."

"All-right, now I want you to put your foot on the brake and turn the key, but leave the car in park for just a moment." I did just as he said. I listened intently, making sure to follow his instructions to the letter. Since I knew everything there was to know about everything, I knew enough to know that I didn't have a car of my own. So, if I was ever going to use my driving skills without supervision, I would eventually have to borrow my parents' car. Hence, I tried to do everything I could to convince my father that I had an inherent, God-given ability with respect to motor vehicle operations. I guess I was pretty successful up to that point, because he then turned to me and said the one sentence that every sixteen-year-old young man with a learner's permit wants to hear.

"O.K. Let's put it into drive."
My hand was grabbing for the gearshift before he could even finish his sentence. I guess he could see the eagerness in my eyes, because he stopped me to give me one last bit of instruction.

"Wait, now. You're still learning, so we're going to take it a little slowly at first. We're going to drive around the parking lot, but remember, in order to move forward you don't have to hit the gas. All you need to do is ease your foot off the brake."

I wish I had known that at the time with this seemingly insignificant statement he was doing much more than teaching me how to drive. I am now much older than sixteen. I went on to graduate from high school and college, got a good job, worked for a while, and then eventually went back to graduate school. So now as I look back, it's interesting to see my progression. When I was sixteen, I thought that I knew everything there was to know about everything. When I graduated from college, I knew that I had gained some additional knowledge since high school. So, then, I was sure that I knew everything about everything, and I had a piece of paper to prove it. I started working a nine-to-five, and for the first time in my life, I realized that I didn't know nothin' about nothin'.

Now that I have a master's degree and am working on a Ph.D., I think I know a little something; but I'm conscious of how much there actually is to know, and how much of it I don't know. I now approach life from that perspective and, as a result, I have been blessed with the aforementioned drive-time epiphanies; and it seems like the older I get, the more of these epiphanies I have. For example, I've conducted several independent research studies on "hanging out" over the past few years. One day while driving to school, I was analyzing the data I collected and concluded that, as my father had told me, there really aren't too many productive things happening in the streets at three o'clock in the morning. I now realize that, believe it or not, there are certain places that I just shouldn't go. There are certain people I shouldn't hang around, no matter how much fun they may appear to be having; and you are, in fact, extremely lucky if you can find one or two people that you can call true friends.

I recently had a drive-time epiphany that was particularly profound. A few years ago, I found out that I was going to be a father. This was totally unplanned and unexpected. I was terrified. First of all, after many years of thinking about it, I had decided that I didn't ever want to have children. I was also very focused on completing my Ph.D. and advancing my career, and I had finally reached the point where

I felt like my life was firing on all cylinders. I was moving, full speed ahead. So, I wasn't sure how I would be able to be a father and still move forward with the things I wanted to do. Finally, I never thought that I had the patience or the temperament for parenthood. So, needless to say, I was decidedly torn and somewhat distraught.

My daughter was born on November 8, 2004. So, during the holidays, I was able to stop for a moment and really take time to enjoy the pleasures that fatherhood brings; and, despite my fears, I've found a way to continue to make progress academically and professionally.

So, as I was driving along one day, during the time that we were putting the finishing touches on this book, I had yet another realization. Even in the face of unexpected challenges, I can still move forward. This book is a perfect example of that forward motion. All I have to do, when faced with a new challenge, is remember three things my father taught me: 1) I should take time to get used to the feel of the driver's seat; 2) I should learn to appreciate the privilege of driving; and 3) In order to move forward, I don't have to hit the gas--all I need to do is ease my foot off the brake. And I'll be darned if the old man wasn't right!

jsg

7. Blind Spot

Every man has a blind spot
Whether he knows it or not
A place where he cannot see
What is coming up on the side
The mirror's rear view
Just can't do
The job of giving clear sight
To the oncoming car or truck
Coming up fast on the right
Sometimes it's mother's name
Sometimes it's sister's shame
Or even daddy's midnight slide
Maybe broken laws
Whatever the cause
He can't just relax
And enjoy the ride
When he's rolling
In the fast lane
Trying to get ahead
Of the game
He realizes it's time
To change lanes
To move toward the exit ramp
Everything's rolling fine
He sees the exit sign
And decides to clamp
Down on the metal pedal
Life's destination is in sight
Turn signal's blinking light
When the horn's blare
And the scowling stare

Of the one he could not see
Blind sided
Off track set back
As he swerves
Toward the curb.

rlg

I ain't your...

That Word

From Mother to Son

What's in a Name?

A Father's Sacrifice

8. That Word (Jephthah's Lament)

N-word, B-word
Mother-, Son-
The dozens game
Is never done
When your guard is down
From too much booze
You play the card
The suit and choose
That word!

I wonder why they say that word aloud
they say it applies to me
I wonder why they say that word aloud
its such a cruelty
'cause I'm me, its all that I can be
and I am free, God has set me free
change my mother,
change my name
change my father too
I am still who I am
tell me who are you?
are you free?
free as you can be?
are you free?
free just like me?

N-word, B-word
Mother-, Son-
The dozens game
Is never won
When you cross the line

You always lose
You can't play the game
Unless you use
That word!

you say my mother was no good
you say she fell from grace
you say my father went outside
his family and his place
but I'm me
its all that I can be
and I'm free
God has set me free

N-word, B-word
Mother-, Son-
The dozens game
Is never fun
When you play the game
You cannot snooze
Your alert opponent
Will always use
That word!

One day when the world is fair
people just like me
can take their place anywhere
in society
and be free,
free as they can be
and be free
God has set them free
are you free?

24

free as you can be
are you free?
free just like ME?

N-word, B-word
Mother-, Son
The dozens game
Is never done
That word!

rlg

9. From Mother to Son

I've been called a mother
And a son
I don't answer to
Either one
Both are mind benders
For one of my gender
When expressed this way
I must stand to say
I am a son
But absolutely no one
Can demean my sense of self
My mother was no saint
But one thing she ain't
Is the B-word
Loosely thrown as an epithet
A cry vulgar and obscene
Designed to demean
And generate the anger
Exceeded only by that
Caused by the
Mother loving word
Its all so absurd
Why we use that word
Whose only purpose
Is to cause one brother
To kill another
Who didn't even
Know his mother

rlg

10. What's in a Name?

I want my name back. I don't really like the name Ronald. It's a good name, given to me by my father and mother. They obviously thought it was a fine name that somehow represented the little wrinkled up newborn that I was. I carried that name for almost twenty years of my life. It was taken from me so subtly and quickly, that I did not realize at first that my name was in jeopardy. I was a nineteen year-old graduate student beginning study on my doctorate in chemistry. The chemistry department held a reception (called a "smoker") for the new graduate fellows and teaching assistants at a bar in the Shadyside section of Pittsburgh. They served pitcher after pitcher of ice cold beer. It looked so good and I was thirsty, though underage. One of the friendly older graduate students said, "Here Ron, let me fill your glass." "Thanks," I responded. "My name is Ronald." "Yes, Ron. I know. It's good to meet you."

I tried again and again during the next few days of orientation to get the accommodating professors and eager graduate students to hear that my name is Ronald. I failed completely. I had become "Ron" by the end of the term. I have often wondered if I gave up too easily.   After all, the implications are cultural and racial.

In the Black community of the 60's south, a young man never shaved his mustache or his name. He either used his full name or the descriptive nickname bestowed by his male peer group or family. I still remember the smirk on the face of my barber when I walked into the shop at fourteen and said proudly, "The usual haircut and trim the mustache please." He lathered my upper lip and scraped his razor around for a minute or two. He then charged me ten cents extra as I left the shop with a big grin on my face.

Most of my northern colleagues--Black and White-have no idea why I keep whining about a name. They have always used the short versions of names with no apparent harm to the man involved. William has always been Bill, and certainly Bartholomew isn't going to argue about being called Bart. I really do understand their point, but I don't believe they realize that this theft of names coincides with the great social upheavals of the sixties that brought an end to segregation and the positive cultural influences that Black professionals exerted on young Black men. A simple incident occurred a few years after I married my college sweetheart that illustrates the great cultural divide on this point. I had gone home to Florida to visit my parents for a few days. My wife had remained in Pittsburgh. She called my parent's house and asked for "Ron." My first cousin who was in his twenties and a graduate of Brown University, answered the phone and said, "There is no one here by that name," as he hung up the phone. My wife, who was sure that she had not mis-dialed, thought for a second and then called back. This time my cousin handed me the phone after she asked, "May I speak to Ronald, please?"

The first name was important, but the last name, the family name, was essential. My brother, who is two years older than I, was known as Glenn by the older boys who were his classmates. He wore the family name proudly. I couldn't wait until I was old enough for this important recognition. The effective and positive use of the last name was so pervasive in the Black college community of that era, that all students were called by last name and given a title. Even as a young freshman at Florida A. and M. University, I was called Mr. Glenn by my teachers. These schools were criticized in some higher education circles for being too formal. That alleged formality, however, placed a significant positive pressure on students to behave in a manner that was worthy of the respect shown to them. This was a subtle application of the biblical principle to "speak those things that are not as though they were."

I had only Black professors in college who taught me that I should think and behave like "Mr. Glenn." I only had white professors in graduate school, who quickly taught me that I was not Mr. Glenn. I wasn't even Ronald anymore. The professors weren't the only ones. The entire society had joined the conspiracy to take and change my name. If I went to the doctor's office, the receptionist explained "Ron, Dr. Blank will see you in a few minutes." When I purchased my first used car, the salesman said, "Thanks Ron, have a good day," as he stamped my check. I noticed a glaring inconsistency in this name-calling business. I could never have a title, but the manager who was allegedly consulted about a better deal on the car was "Mr. Manager."

I wonder sometimes how our young men would behave if they were given a title joined to a last name that carried the full import of the family heritage when they were still young, and before they had done anything to deserve the honor, other than being born Black and male.

rlg

11. A Father's Sacrifice

And Jephthah made a vow to the LORD: "If you give the Ammonites into my hands, whatever comes out of the door of my house to meet me when I return in triumph from the Ammonites will be the LORD'S, and I will sacrifice it as a burnt offering." (Judges 11:30-31).

There was a time when people were very concerned about how to worship God so that God would be pleased and accept their offerings. Most people thought that God was a God of wrath, waiting for them to make a misstep so that God could bring down the hammer on their heads and punish them. When they thought about God, they saw someone who did indeed sit high and look low, trying to find a way to condemn people. Worship, therefore, was more about how to appease this angry God than praise. So, people decided that human beings needed to find the right rituals, ceremonies, and sacrifices in order to please God.

Israelites looked at the other countries, nations, and tribes around them to find out how they worshiped their gods. They noticed that they all made sacrifices and observed that the priests and the prophets sometimes beat themselves with chains or cut themselves with knives. In the most extreme cases, when everything else had failed, they would make the highest sacrifice and kill their own precious children.

After the death of Joshua, the people were without leadership until somebody felt a special anointing through the Spirit of God to lead the people in the time of great danger. The people would pray and select a "charismatic leader of the holy war," a judge who would leave his or her normal occupation and lead the army of God against the enemy.

The story of Jephthah, one of the judges, is told in chapters 11 and 12 of the book of Judges. Jephthah was a bastard. That's a rude word, but descriptive of his situation. Jephthah's father was a well respected married man who had an adulterous relationship with a neighbor that led to Jephthah's birth. Jephthah was not well liked by his other brothers. They called him names because he was not legitimate like the rest of them. Even though Jephthah grew up to be a very strong person physically, mentally and spiritually, they drove him away because of the circumstances of his birth. He went off into another country where he became a great warrior who distinguished himself on the field of battle. He was strong in character and faith, a charismatic and just warrior-leader.

The time came that Israel found itself facing great danger from a terrifying enemy on the horizon. The people sent a delegation to Jephthah to remind him that he was one of them, of the same flesh. They begged him to come back and be the judge over them and lead them in the holy war.

Sometimes in life you may be called to go back home to the same ones who looked down their noses at you and were not kind to you. Your human response, understandably, would be to tell them where they could go to find help and to remind them of all the things that they used to say about you, your mother, and father. As Jesus said, a prophet is not without honor, except in his own country, among his own kin. But when the Spirit of the Lord is on you; when God is in the mix, your response has to be like that of Jephthah. Jephthah reminded them how they used to treat him but he felt that God was calling him to go back to his people and lead them in this confrontation with the Ammonites. *Jephthah then returned in his own strength and in his own power, but the Spirit of God was on him.* (Judges 11:29).

However, Jephthah made one mistake. He held on to an ancient idea about who God was. God had given Jephthah the ability to be very strong. He was a wise military leader, but he still was not sure that God was going to give him the victory. He had seen what all the other neighboring people did in order to get close to their gods. So, he did something that a lot of us still do today. He tried to bargain with God. Sometimes when we face the big problems in life, some of us will say to God, "Let's make a deal!" Jephthah said, "*Lord, if you give me this victory then whatever comes out of my door when I come back in victory, I will sacrifice it as a burnt offering.*" (Judges 11:30-31). God had already assured the victory. No deal was necessary. When God calls you from what you were to what you are going to be, God has already made the arrangements.

You know the rest of the story. They went off to war and won the victory. His only daughter was so happy that Daddy had won the victory and was coming home that she was the first to come rushing out of the house to meet him. I have often wondered at what moment it came back into his memory that he had made a vow to the Lord? Was it when he saw her or was he so caught up in the exhilaration of the moment that he didn't realize it right then?

Jephthah rose above his own father's failures to become a loving father to his only daughter. He failed, however, to understand his heavenly Father. Jephthah made a vow to the Lord, and thought that he could not change it. "I made a vow," he said to his daughter. This young virgin woman said to her father, "*You have given your word to the Lord. Do to me just as you promised, now that the Lord has avenged you of your enemies, the Ammonites.*" (Judges 11:36). Many writers disagree about what Jephthah did. Some argue that her father did not really kill her. Instead, they suggest, she had to remain a perpetual virgin who could never get married. Others say he killed his daughter and burned her body on an altar as a sacrifice because he felt that he could not repent of his vow.

Men can learn much from Jephthah's story. First, we, like Jephthah, will often have to forgive those who have mistreated us in order to do what God calls us to do. Second, we must remember that our actions often affect those closest to us. Therefore, we must carefully examine situations before making promises that we may regret. Third, we must develop our own understanding of God because the beliefs of others may fail us.

Had Jephthah lived many years later, he could have benefited from the experience of Nicodemus. Nicodemus, a Jewish leader, sneaked into the place where an itinerant preacher named Jesus was staying. He came at night because he did not want other folks to see him because he was a big shot in the community. He probably had been to the seminaries and the universities and may have earned his Ph.D. He wanted to talk with Jesus because he had heard about the miracles that Jesus had done and all the signs that pointed to him as the Messiah sent from God. Jesus explained that Nicodemus could not understand what he was preaching unless he was born again and underwent a radical change in the way that he thought about God. God is not sitting in heaven looking for ways to condemn errant human beings. In fact, Jesus said, "God so loved the world that he gave his only son..." (John 3:16). He taught Nicodemus that God's attitude toward creation is love. No animals, children, or even grain needed to be sacrificed. God provided and would accept the only sacrifice required.

rlg

All that looks dumb, ain't

Hip Hop is Not Dead

Stolen Minds

12. Hip Hop is Not Dead

On the first day of the week we came together to break bread. Paul spoke to the people and, because he intended to leave the next day, kept on talking until midnight. There were many lamps in the upstairs room where we were meeting. Seated in a window was a young man named Eutychus, who was sinking into a deep sleep as Paul talked on and on. When he was sound asleep, he feel to the ground from the third story and was picked up dead. Paul went down, threw himself on the young man and put his arms around him. "Don't be alarmed," he said. "He's alive!" (Acts 20:7-11).

Webster's Dictionary defines a generation as a group of individuals born and living contemporaneously. The word contemporaneous means existing, occurring, or originating during the same time. In society we often define a generation not only as a group of people who exist at the same time, but a group of people who reach their formative years, or make the transition into adulthood around the same period of time. The time span used to define a generation is centered on some event or group of events. In the history books you may read about the World War I generation or the World War II generation. My parents belonged to the Baby Boomer Generation. The Baby Boomer Generation consists of people born between the years of 1946 and the early 1960's. They are called the Baby Boomers because 1946 marks the end of World War II. This is a significant time because at the end of the war, you had many American service men returning home after being away from their wives for a long time. As a result, husbands and wives got together and started having a whole lot of babies. There was a sharp increase in the number of babies being born, or a baby boom. This generation of people is often described as strong and resourceful and hard working.

Much of this generation came of age during the height of the civil rights struggle in America.

The generation born between the early 1960's and the mid to late 1970's is called Generation X. We call this Generation X because the letter X is often used to represent a variable or some unknown quantity. The people of this generation began making the transition into adulthood during the Cold War. It was called a cold war because there were no guns being fired. There were no bombs going off, but Russia and the United States were storing up all of these weapons for a possible war against each other. The children of this generation came up during the eighties when there was an economic recession and many people were out of work. There was a lot of uncertainty during their formative years and this group was in turn uncertain about what to do with their lives and had no sense of direction. Consequently, they were labeled Generation X.

I was born on August 6, 1977, which was at the tail end of the time frame for Generation X. Some might even say that I was born a little bit too late to be considered part of Generation X. However, around the time that I was born, there was a new movement in music. It was a genre of music that had never been heard before. Instead of vocalists singing over smooth melodies, people called M.C.'s talked in rhyming phrases over break beats. Some of the younger readers might think that hip hop, or rap music, has been around forever, but this is a relatively new form of music. Along with the music came an entirely new evolving culture that affected the way people spoke, danced, and even dressed. This movement has continued to gain momentum and is now a dominant force in popular culture. Hip Hop artists are selling the most albums. They influence the clothing styles. They star in movies. This musical genre greatly affects American culture in every way. One could make the argument that the young people of today, people around my age and younger, have almost been defined by this movement called hip-hop and everything that comes with it. We are the Hip Hop Generation. Since hip hop is not only a genre of music, but also a culture of people, some might even say that we are hip hop. Many people, especially people of other generations, see hip hop music as a type of music that has no lasting value. Furthermore, they believe that we, the Hip Hop Generation, have no redeeming qualities.

Most of the people reading this book belong to one of the generations I described. Each generation has something very different that defines it. So the question becomes how do we bridge the generational divide? As a member of the Hip Hop Generation, I can identify with a passage in the twentieth chapter of Acts that I'm going to use to suggest some solutions. Acts focuses a lot on Paul and his work and travels. One evening as he was preaching with the intention of leaving town the next day, a young man named Eutychus was present in the congregation. I picture Eutychus as a member of the hip hop generation of his day. He was walking around with baggy pants and Timberlands. He has his do rag on and his baggy FUBU shirt. His grandma had yanked him by the arm and said, "Come on boy! We gon' go down to that church down the street and listen to Paul preach." And so Eutychus went.

Now, here is one interesting thing that you should note. Once Eutychus got to the little church down the street, where did he sit? He sat on a window sill. If you go into any building where are the windows located? They are located on the outside walls of the building. So, Eutychus was in the building, but he was sitting on the window sill, just barely inside.

Paul had a certain reputation that preceded him. Paul was a very knowledgeable person who was always trying to wrestle with and grow in his faith. He was in the business of trying to convert people to Christianity and truly make disciples. We see in this passage that Paul was a long-winded preacher whose sermons probably got a little boring at times. In the passage, Paul said, "I have to leave early in the morning and I might not see you for a while, so I'm going to keep you until midnight so I can tell you everything that I think you might want to hear." Now we have a clear picture of the setting. The young man, Eutychus, a member of the Hip Hop Generation, was sitting on the very edge of the room. I imagine that he might not even have been able to hear everything Paul was saying because he was so far away from the action. He listened to Paul talk on and on until he fell asleep and tumbled from the third story of the building.

We sometimes create the circumstances for such a thing to happen in the church. We take the members of the Hip Hop Generation, drag them into church and force them to sit on the outskirts, way up in the window sill. They might not be physically on the outskirts of the church, but they can sit on the front pew and still be mentally on the window sill. Many churches do a good job of bringing young people in and getting them involved, but even in those churches there are still some young people, some members of the Hip Hop Generation, sitting on the window sill. Not only that, but if we don't involve them in the affairs of the church; if we don't speak to them in a language that they understand; if we don't find a way to make the church experience interesting for them; if we don't involve them in activities in which they want to participate; they will get bored and fall asleep. Once they are sleeping it is so much easier for them to fall.

The second thing that I think you should note is that when Eutychus did fall, the people stood by and watched while Paul knelt down, threw himself on the young man and covered him. Paul was able to bridge the generational gap and see that there was still life in Eutychus because he was not afraid to get up close to him. Other people were there, but the text implies that the other people were just standing around watching and saying to each other, "I just saw the boy fall three stories. There's no way anybody could survive a fall like that. He wasn't moving. I didn't see him breathing. He must be dead." We can see that everyone must have assumed that he was dead because Paul had to announce and proclaim that Eutychus was, in fact, alive. We have the same problem today in the church. We see young people fall all the time, and we proclaim them to be dead. We say things like, "That Billy stays in trouble with the law. He is not doing well in school and is always walking around with his pants hanging half off his butt, listening to that rap music all the time..." or we say, "Susie ain't nothing but a fast little girl. She went out and got pregnant." We see that they have fallen and proclaim them dead!

The question is, do you get up close? Do you get close to them and cover them like Paul did? Do you cover them with your love? Do you cover them with your kindness? Do you cover them with your time and your attention? Do you cover them with the same love that Christ uses to cover you? If you do, you will be able to see that even the members of the Hip Hop Generation; even those of us who have fallen the farthest and hit the ground the hardest, still have life in us. The crowd stood at a distance and said Eutychus is not breathing, but Paul got down on the ground with him, on his hands and knees, and bent over him, and put his cheek to Eutychus' mouth and felt the breath on his cheek. Though it may have been a faint breath, he was able to say definitively, there is still life in him. I would like to direct this last point to the young people, although it applies to everyone. It's a very simple point. It may almost seem trite, but it is beautiful in its simplicity. Young people, fellow members of the Hip Hop Generation, always remember, just because you have fallen, you don't have to stay there and die. All who you see around you, members of every generation, have fallen at some point in time. Everyone who has gotten up and lived to tell about it, has had someone like Paul to cover them and see the life in them. Paul might be your mother, your father, your grandmother, or a friend. Sometimes Paul might not come in human form at all. So even if you don't have a Paul that you can physically touch, you do not have to lie there and die, because Paul can come in the form of your Heavenly Father, the One who created Paul. Paul can come in the form of the One who comforted Paul, the Holy Spirit. Paul can come in the form of the One who taught Paul, the One who saved Paul, your Lord and Savior, Jesus Christ. With that knowledge, not only should you believe that you do not have to lie there and die, you should refuse to die, because we all have a Paul in our lives.

Remember not the sins of my youth and my rebellious ways; according to your love remember me, for you are good, O LORD. (Psalm 25:7).

jsg

13. Stolen Minds

There was a time
When the minds
Of the young
Were training to take their place
Straining to win the race
Of life
Struggling to end the strife
Between ignorance and wisdom
Knowing that there really is one
Main difference between
Life and death
That spans the breadth
Of tentative uncertainties
Told to be better
Than the other fella
Not just sliding by
Like me
The scholar was a superstar
Praised from near and far
The girls even looked his way
The quarterback got no more play
Than the student who was so smart
The little boy
With the high-water pants
And the white socks
Was given a chance
He was going to be a doctor
The community had so decreed
They would not allow otherwise
Would help to meet his need
If he faltered they held his arms

Or sounded the alarm
The prophecy would be fulfilled
Momentary distractions could not win the day
Reticent reactions could not even sway
His mind from his holy call
Even if the others fall
They call him nerd now
As they herd now
To follow the latest shallow rap
And throw their brains into the mind gap
When did our sisters become ho ho's and bees?
Good only to play bad on their knees
When did our scholars become White wannabees
And stop believing in being the best
Doubting that they can pass the test
Any test of the mind not brawn
Any test that demands a strong
Sense of self and pride
Any test that won't let them hide
From the challenge of mental
Gymnastics instead of simple
Elastic physical maneuvers
Dr. Carver would turn in his grave
Dr. King would rise up to save
The young from the dumbed down life
That dishonors their years of strife

rlg

Roots

Where You From?

H.N.I.C.

In the Woodpile

The Remedy

14. Where You From?

A few years ago, I accompanied my wife when she delivered a paper on Science Education at a gathering of educators in Columbus, Ohio. One of the speakers, a woman from West Virginia whose name I do not recall, read a poem called "Where You From" during one of the breaks. I was struck by the poem and recall thinking everyone should write a poem about where they are from. I don't know whether the speaker wrote the poem herself, but her words so inspired me that the poem below was penned.

So he got up, took the child and his mother during the night and left for Egypt, where he stayed until the death of Herod. And so was fulfilled what the Lord had said through the prophet: "Out of Egypt I called my son." (Matthew 2:14-15).

Where you from?
>   I don't mean just what street
>   Though it would be neat to know
>   Did you have to prime the pump
>   To make the water flow
>   Or carry it from the stream
>   Along the wooded path
>   If you planned to take
>   Your Saturday night bath
Where you from?
>   When you go home
>   No more to roam
>   When you settle down
>   In front of the kettle round the fire
>   With the heart-warming soup

That sticks to the bones
Where you from?
When you eat your first meal
Of the day
Does it include eggs
That the hen lay
Scrambled or fried
Because you tried
To prolong the stay
Of the guests at your table,
Were there grits at that breakfast meal
To satisfy the appeal
Of the man of the house
For a real starter meal
Where you from?
When the family re-unites
After long airplane flights
Do they travel South
Or North or West
Or is the East the place they rest
Where you from?
Did your Mama and daddy grow
A dozen farm hands so
They could bring the crop in on time
Or was the project home
With walls of brick and stone
Or an apartment over the five and dime
When you went to school
Did you act like a fool
And pretend that studying was not cool
Was your life as a scholar
Designed to follow
The paths blazoned
By the intellects of old

Where you from?
    Was your history told
    And the story known
    Of the heroes past
    Who lived in your home
    Were those who looked like you
    Given respectful due
    Or displaced by honor
    Given to others
Where you from?
    Was your home across the tracks
    Forcing you to rush back to
    The safety of familiar grounds
    Did you run like steer and cattle
    To avoid the battle
    And return to your surrounds
    Before the sun went down
Where you from?
    When you worshiped God
    Was it very hard
    To hear the word proclaimed
    Did the tambourines and drums
    Loudly overcome
    The sound preaching in God's name
    Was the service quiet and sedate
    So one could meditate
    On the preacher's gentle homily
    Did the choir and ushers strut
    After the doors were shut
    To start the gospel jamboree
Where you from?
    Was the square
    Your kind of dance
    Maybe the two-step gave you a chance

To hold the one you loved
Real close
Without the looks
That disapproved
Where you from?
Is the land up high
On the mountaintop
Or flat and low
Where the river drops
Down into the valley
Are the streets wide lanes
Or narrow alleys
Slithering between steel and glass
Towers of strength
That run the length
Of the city wide
Or did you run in meadows
In the countryside
Did the sun burn
Your paling hide
Until the hue was dusky
Did you labor in mills
Midst steel and rusty
Metal sheds
Where you from?
When you long for home
Where does your mind roam
Tell me true
So I can know you
Where you from?

rlg

15. H.N.I.C.

In contrast to the stereotype
Against all of the hype
Black men are taught
To have ambition
They do want to strive
To be more than jive
In fact most have
Made the decision
To be the best
That they can be
That is, the H.N.I.C.
Of their house
Or gang
The truth let's tell
Their prison cell
It's a herd mentality
That drives this quest
Not to simply be the best
The heights to which you can go
When you become C.E.O.
Davis, Ossie that is
Called him Deputy for the Colored
Because he had uncovered
The secret to the control
Of Black men's souls
Is to keep them striving
For merely surviving
Not to be the best
Of all the rest
But the best of the
Colored

Black
Negroes
"N" word
Its all so absurd
To accept the limitation
Imposed by a racist nation
That all I can be
Is H.N.I.C.

rlg

16. In the Woodpile

Miscegenation
Discrimination
Transformation
Of the nation
N-word in the woodpile
High yellow
Fellow
Baggy pants style
Members of the class
That's trying to pass
When it seems that
All is pure
You can never be sure
Whose in the
Woodpile
What's really in the file
There might be an N-word
In the woodpile
Three generations down
Sometimes
We can even find
A kind
Of genetic mutation

rlg

17. The Remedy

You know
The unified theory of everything is
Trapped inside the mind
Of some dude slagin' dope on the corner
Yet as space and time erode
We let his brain implode
From the enormous gravity of Bling Theory
But you don't hear me

You know
The key to world peace is
Trapped inside the mind
Of some dude slagin' dope on the corner
But we've convinced ourselves
That the only thing for which we can hope
Is that he'll drop the rocks
Pick up a mic
Spit rhymes over beats
Sell out a few venues
Make enough money
To buy a Bentley
And decide to pay his taxes
Like that's enough not to knock the world off its axis

You know
The cure for cancer is
Trapped inside the mind
Of some dude slagin' dope on the corner
Wasting away amidst so-called urban decay
But that's too obtuse a concept
For you or me to hold

We're not even cajoled by
The tears of a family
Standing by their mother's bedside
In hospice
As she slips in and out of consciousness
And they pray
Guilt-ridden prayers
That if their God still exists
He might take her away
Maybe I'll see
The day when his knowledge can be unlocked
Set free
But that's too big a task for just me
So I'll send these radical thoughts on sabbatical
Set sail down the mainstream
Float slowly past solutions
And add to the pollution

jsg

Look at our world, people

The Snitch

Playground

Who's Next?

Traveling Mercies

18. The Snitch

She was shot two times
And so was he
She in both breasts
And he in the knees
He survived
She didn't see another day
The bass rhythm pounded
As the car drove away
Just another dead ho
Another dead bitch
Witnesses gone blind
They ain't no snitch
She was one of mine
My daughter of ten
They don't care
She's not their kin
The thing that's important
Now this is the hitch
Witnesses gone blind
They ain't no snitch
No police, no sheriff
No F.B.I.
When our cherished
Little children die
At the hands of coward thugs
Who don't even try to hide
Their scowling mugs
They saw her shattered body
As it fell into the ditch
Witnesses gone blind
They ain't no snitch

She was my baby girl
She was all my world
If it takes 'til my dying day
I guarantee that he will pay
The full complete price
For his awful vice
Of the deadly kind
When he killed one of mine
You don't have to snitch
You don't have to tell
I've come to end the lunacy
I am the hound of hell
Since I can't have justice
For my little girl
I can only seek vengeance
On you who stopped her world
Witnesses gone blind
Need to change their mind
Or it will be yours
Next time

rlg

19. Playground

The playground used to be
A place to play games
And swing high
And fast until you almost
Looped around
And flew to land with both
Feet on the ground
Climbed the stairs to the top
Of the slide
And slid so smooth
That the heat of the metal
Absorbing the sun
Scorched your leg and
Burned your behind
Just enough to remind
You that
You really are alive
To do more than
Merely survive
Until you return to
The playground
That had the merry-go-round
Where you could run
As fast as you could
And even Momma wouldn't say stop
As you went round and round and
Jumped when the circular ride ended
Then the young bloods came
And put an end to the games
And carefree days of early evening fun
We now leave with the departing sun

And Momma won't let us come
To the playground by ourselves
Or with our friends
And certainly not alone
Those days are gone
No amount of pleading or begging smiles
Can change our fear of those whose styles
Are menacing
Their hands touch
One open one closed
Just so much
That the exchange is made
And men drive by
With darkened shades
Hidden passengers
Making new roads in the grass
Behind the garbage bins
At the playground
Where no one can see the sins
Going down
The teeter-totter let you enjoy
The ups and downs of life
If the kid on the other side
Was not too big and nice
Enough not to jump off
When his side was down
That's why I miss the playground
As I look through the bars
On my living room window
And search the channels with
The remote control that
Unleashes the shows
As I sit behind
The bolted doors

And try to find some joy
With a broken, faded toy
And the games I play in
The playground of my mind.

rlg

20. Who's Next?

I hate to stand in line
At the bank or at the store
Especially when there are
Two or three or more
Ahead of me in line
It's not waiting my turn
That I mind
So much as the certainty
That when there is finally
No one ahead of me
The teller or the cashier
Will say to no one in particular
While barely glancing my way
"Who's next?"
Or if she is more verbose
She'll look at the white person
Who is most close
And seek permission to wait on me
From this closest white
She can see
"May I help whose next?"
The small talk that she tries to make
Is much too small to take
The sting out of this
Directed slight
As I stand within her line of sight
Imagined headlines loudly glare
"Crazy Negro Dumps His Wares"
All over the counter
With a loud plea
I'm next damn it!
Wait on me!

rlg

21. Traveling Mercies

Love must be sincere. Hate what is evil; cling to what is good. Be devoted to one another in brotherly love. Honor one another above yourselves. (Romans 12:9-10).

As the time approached for him to be taken up to heaven, Jesus resolutely set out for Jerusalem. And he sent messengers on ahead, who went into a Samaritan village to get things ready for him; but the people there did not welcome him, because he was heading for Jerusalem. When the disciples James and John saw this, they asked, "Lord, do you want us to call fire down from heaven to destroy them?" But Jesus turned and rebuked them, and they went to another village. (Luke 9:51-56).

Jesus was an itinerant preacher who was always on the move. This chapter is about the last journey that Jesus and his disciples made to Jerusalem. It is included here because it demonstrates how men must learn to trust each other by overcoming the natural fear that they feel. Jesus and his disciples were up north in comfortable familial surroundings and preparing to travel one last time into the southern regions that included Jerusalem. Jesus directed his disciples to arrange for every stage of the trip. *And he sent messengers on ahead, who went into a Samaritan village to get things ready for him. (Luke 9:52).*

There was a slight problem with their travel itinerary. Jewish pilgrims traveling to Jerusalem did not usually pass through Samaria. However, in order to get from the north to the south in the fastest time, the travel plans involved passing through the territory of the Samaritans. The Samaritans were related to the Jews but considered to be impure. Their ancestors included the conquering Assyrian colonists who, some thought, had polluted the Jewish genetic pool with their unclean blood. Comparisons with the mulatto offspring of southern American slave holders would not be farfetched. Furthermore, they had different ways of worshiping God since they held Mt. Gerazim to be sacred instead of Jerusalem that was so beloved by pure Jews. The enmity between Jews and Samaritans was so great that the biblical description of the reaction of the Samaritans is not surprising--"*the people there did not welcome him, because he was heading for Jerusalem.*" *(Luke 9:53).* This trip was not off to a good start.

Jesus' twelve disciples included two, James and John, who were known as the "Sons of Thunder". They were not about to take this affront lightly. They knew how to deal with such insolent, disrespectful people. They threw their angry question at Jesus, "*Lord, do you want us to call fire down from heaven to destroy them?*" *(Luke 9:54).* Their reaction was very human and understandable. Jesus' response to them must have felt like a stinging slap on the face. Jesus rebuked them. They were not the ones who insulted the Master, yet he rebuked them. Jesus was trying to tell them that in him God was doing a new work like none before. The old way said hate your enemies. The new commandment was to love everyone. The old idea was vengeance for every slight. The new idea was to turn the other cheek.

Moreover, this particular Samaritan village did miss a tremendous opportunity because Jesus told his disciples to go on to another (Samaritan) village. He was on his way to Jerusalem to die, to fulfill God's promise. He did not have time for confrontations that might delay his rendezvous with destiny. He needed his disciples to move beyond the natural fear and distrust of people who are not like them.

Jesus wanted his disciples to have such spiritual insight that when he left them physically they would be able to do what he had called them to do. He taught, "*If your brother sins against you, go and show him his fault, just between the two of you.*"

If he listens to you, you have won your brother over." (Matthew 18:15) That's tough for a lot of us to do. The hardest conversations that we have are those that just involve two people--you and that other person. It is usually easier to stand before a great crowd or even before a world-wide television audience. Jesus said that if she or he listens, you've won that person over. If he or she doesn't listen then you have to get some others involved.

Jesus said to the disciples, *"Whatever you bind on earth will be bound in heaven, and whatever you loose on earth will be loosed in heaven." (Matthew 18:18).* He added, *"If two of you on earth agree about anything you ask for, it will be done for you by my Father in Heaven." (Matthew 18:19).* James and John must have been thinking, "But Lord, we agree that you should nuke these disrespectful half-breed Samaritans." Like so many Christians, they had only considered part of what Jesus was saying. He had also said, *"For where two or three come together in my name, there am I with them." (Matthew 18:20).* "My name" means in love, so that somehow one must find a way to move beyond the things that divide and be united by the love of Christ. Paul explains that, *"love must be sincere." (Romans 12:9).* Love has to be real; there's no phoniness in this love.

Mealtimes often force us to get very close and even lean on or touch each other. Near the end of their journey Jesus and his disciples shared a special meal together. The Bible tells us that while they were eating Jesus took bread, gave thanks, broke it and gave it to his disciples and said *"Take, eat, this is my body." (Mark 14:22).* Most of us can quote that scripture. We hear it every Communion Sunday, and we think we know what it means. Jesus was still trying to get the disciples to a level of spiritual understanding. He wanted them to learn through this ritual meal that they must be bound together by their love for him and each other. There could not be divisions among them with each one claiming spiritual independence from the others. They were reclining around the table, a low table that forced diners to lean on the adjacent person. It wasn't possible to sit at that meal and not invade the space of the ones who were near.

I am reminded of a dear sister in a church where I was the pastor many years ago who always waited until everyone else had finished praying during the altar call before she went up to pray. She knelt alone without the possibility of touching or being touched by anyone else. That's not the way it was at that disciples' last meal with Jesus. It was an intimate gathering of thirteen men around a table. Modern day men have a real problem getting that close to each other. Spiritual independence, contrary to what one may think, requires that sometimes we must get close to those who are part of this same spiritual circumstance. We can't push them away. We need to draw them close, and that's why Jesus required that we must talk to the ones who sin against us and show them their fault.

Holiday weekends are times of travel for many people in the United States. A common prayer request as each journey begins is for "traveling mercies." We pray that God will grant us a successful journey to our destination and a safe return to our homes. My wife and I traveled by train to Florida a few years ago. We were six and one-half hours late getting back to Washington, DC from Jacksonville, Florida; six and one-half hours! On the way down we arrived in Jacksonville so late that we missed the train to Tallahassee, our final destination. We decided to go to the bus station and catch a bus from Jacksonville to Tallahassee late at night.

Riding a bus is a fascinating experience today. If you want to see America, go down to the bus station and look. We rushed to the bus station to catch the bus which was very crowded. We asked the ticket seller if there were seats on the bus. She said that she did not have the foggiest notion; she just sold the tickets. If there were not enough seats, the company would add another bus. With that assurance, we rushed to get on the bus. It was eleven o'clock at night, and people had sacked out for the night for this last trip. There were not two adjacent seats where my wife and I could sit together but we had our ticket and we were on the bus. The driver said, "Alright you folks who have luggage on the seats, you either have to buy another ticket or remove your luggage from the seat because there are people getting on here and they need to sit down."

We moved on back until we passed by one place where there was one empty seat and one man who was stretched out across both seats. He looked up at me with a less than friendly look that dared me to sit down. I told my wife to take the single seat in the next row while I summoned the nerve to sit next to this dear brother. He moved an inch or two, just enough to let me know that he had moved though he really didn't want to move. I squeezed into that little space and sat very still. I was so much aware that we were in close proximity to each other. We must get close to our companions and often close to strangers who we meet along the way when traveling. I didn't want to move because if I accidentally touched him he might consider that an assault on his manhood. That could have been just what it would take to drive him off the deep end to make the newspaper headline the next day. Every now and then he would shift around a little bit as if trying to nudge me even further toward the arm rest. We were close. We had no choice. We didn't know each other. It was quite uncomfortable for me. At one point he shifted his body so that his knee hit up against me. The contact was subtle but definite. "It's all about to come out now," I thought. I braced myself for the anticipated verbal assault from this groggy, hostile stranger. But, when he realized that he had accidentally bumped against me, he did something that reminded me of what Jesus had said. This wasn't a longtime relationship. This was a momentary communication between two strangers. He said two words, "Excuse me."

These two simple words diverted my thoughts to a totally different path and made me understand what Romans 12: 9-10 and Luke 9:51-56 are about. I was reminded that Jesus was telling us that we have to recognize the humanness and personhood of everyone. I was convicted because I had formed judgments about somebody that I didn't even know and caused so much unnecessary tension as I rode along. We Christians have to understand that Jesus said that if our brother sins against us, we must communicate with each other in Christ.

Jesus said that he would not drink again of this cup until he could drink it in the Kingdom of God. When will that kingdom come? It will come when those who say they are Christians are able to understand that one of the things they have to do in life, when they encounter strangers, is to be able to say "excuse me." If the other person offers the excuse, we must be able to accept the apology with grace and love. The Kingdom of God is that place where the loving will of God rules. That means the love of God binds us more than the fear of each other separates us.

We continued to ride in silence toward Tallahassee to complete the three hours, fifteen minutes and twenty-two seconds of the journey. The trip was uneventful except for what I would call my "spiritual epiphany" and my numb leg and foot. I ended the final stage of the trip with my traditional prayer of thanks to God. I also made a vow to God. I know very well that when one makes a vow, it is good to plan to keep it. My vow to God was, "Thank you so much for bringing us safely though this lengthy train and bus ride experience; and if it's in my ability and power, it's not an experience that I intend to have again in this life." I was reassured that God is merciful. God is gracious. God will provide all of our spiritual needs throughout this journey called life if we take the time to receive the benefits of "traveling mercies."

rlg

An awesome God

Flirting with the Master

The Father Who Wanted More

After Thanksgiving

22. Flirting with the Master

"Sir," the woman said, "I can see that you are a prophet. Our fathers worshiped on this mountain, but you Jews claim that the place where we must worship is in Jerusalem." Jesus declared, "Believe me, woman, a time is coming when you will worship the Father neither on this mountain nor in Jerusalem. You Samaritans worship what you do not know; we worship what we do know, for salvation is from the Jews. Yet a time is coming and has now come when the true worshipers will worship the Father in spirit and truth, for they are the kind of worshipers the Father seeks. God is spirit, and his worshipers must worship in spirit and in truth." (John 4:19-24).

This scripture presents an intriguing situation. Jesus had just finished performing miracles and engaging his disciples in a theological discussion about the true way to obtain salvation and gain eternal life. They were on their way back home to Galilee. Jesus decided to leave Judea because he learned that the Pharisees were spreading the news that he had more converts than John the Baptist. *The Pharisees heard that Jesus was gaining and baptizing more disciples than John, although it was not Jesus who baptized but his disciples. When the Lord learned of this he left Judea and went back once more to Galilee. (John 4:1-3).* When he left Judea to return to Galilee, it was a strategic retreat. Jesus was keenly aware of his disciples' inflated egos and probably decided to take them away from the talk of the Pharisees about John's smaller number of baptisms. Since the disciples were the ones actually doing the baptizing, they might have become distracted from their true mission of saving souls and become caught up in the unimportant fact that they were doing better than their dearly beloved John the Baptist. We men often get pulled into ego-assaulting "mine is bigger than yours" arguments. Jesus quickly averted any possibility of that happening by deciding to return home.

They had to pass through Samaria in order to get home. They came to Jacob's well, where they took a break, because they were tired from the long journey. It was about noon when Jesus sat by the well while the disciples went to town to get provisions. A woman came near to draw water. She was a Samaritan who despite some Jewish blood in her veins, was not regarded as being pure. Moreover, she was a woman who apparently was not reluctant to talk with a strange man. Jesus asked her for a drink. He must have been quite a sight to her inquisitive eyes with his nappy hair, dark skin and a nice robe, looking like the pure Jew that he was. She had flirted with men before, but this time she was inadvertently flirting with the Master. She must have thought, "You people don't normally have anything to do with us and certainly not a woman of my status."

In fact, she and Jesus had a discussion about water and life--the life she had lived and the abundant life that this strange man offered. Jesus knew things about her legal and illicit relationships with men. Her casual flirtatiousness ended as she realized that she was speaking with a man like no other man she had ever met. "Maybe he is a prophet," she thought, because he had so much special and intimate knowledge about her.

Then she decided to show him that she, too, knew a little something. She knew the right way to worship God. She told the prophet that she knew that God should be worshiped on this mountain, not down in Jerusalem as the Jews insisted. Jesus told the Samaritan woman, *"Believe me, woman, a time is coming when you will worship the Father neither on this mountain nor in Jerusalem....God is spirit and his worshippers must worship in spirit and in truth." (John 4:21, 24).* God had taken this simple circumstance and allowed it to provide an opportunity to make one of the greatest theological arguments that we find in the Bible. There were those who believed that God must be worshiped in a great cathedral or temple. There were those who asserted that one must go high up on the mountain to find God. Some sought God down in the valley or out in the wilderness. Jesus explained to this woman that God is a Spirit and will not be confined to a location in space and time.

Another message embedded in Jesus' encounter with the woman at the well is a reiteration of what Jesus spoke about following the time when he was approached by Nicodemus who came to Jesus at night. *(John3:2)*. It was not customary for a woman to be seen openly talking to a strange man. Even in today's society, men have a difficult time talking to women openly. However, Jesus did not have a problem breaking that cultural rule to converse with this woman in the broad daylight. The following scripture puts Jesus' actions in perspective. *"This is the verdict: Light has come into the world, but men loved darkness instead of light because their deeds were evil. Everyone who does evil hates the light, and will not come into the light for fear that his deeds will be exposed. But whoever lives by the truth comes into the light, so that it may be seen plainly that what he has done has been done through God." (John 3:19-21)*. Men, there is no shame or need to hide in the darkness if your conversation with a woman is honorable and done in a respectful manner. Jesus showed that men can rise above the flirtatiousness of some women and respond to them in a more meaningful, godly way. He used this encounter to minister to her on a spiritual level that transformed, what might have been fleshly intentions, into a profound understanding of God and her new being in Christ.

So, out of that theological tension between the "pure" and the "impure", the "complete" and the "incomplete", Jesus took the opportunity to explain the nature of God and God's people to the men and women who were responsible for the founding and preservation of the Christian church. The spiritual foundation of the church rests on this man who had a conversation by the well with a flirtatious woman. He opened her eyes and ours to a new understanding of who God is. God expects from us, even to this day, nothing but the truth.   rlg

23. The Father Who Wanted More

One of the men in the crowd spoke up and said, "Teacher, I brought my son for you to heal him. He can't speak because he is possessed by an evil spirit that won't let him talk. And whenever this evil spirit seizes him, it throws him violently to the ground and makes him foam at the mouth and grind his teeth and become rigid. So I asked your disciples to cast out the evil spirit, but they couldn't do it." (Mark 9:17-18).

Afterward the disciples asked Jesus privately, "Why couldn't we cast out that demon?" "You didn't have enough faith," Jesus told them. "I assure you, even if you had faith as small as a mustard seed you could say to this mountain, 'Move from here to there,' and it would move. Nothing would be impossible." (Matthew 17:19-20).

You probably remember this story about a father whose son had an ailment described as demon possession. He brought his son to Jesus' disciples while Jesus was away. They failed to heal the young man. The father cried to Jesus, *"But if you can do anything, take pity on us and help us." (Mark 9:22).* Jesus answered, *"Everything is possible for him who believes." (Mark 9:23).* The boy's father exclaimed, *"I do believe; help me overcome my unbelief!" (Mark 9:24).* The father's cry really was, "I have some faith, but I want more."

Jesus was known for his ability to heal. We're not really surprised that a parent took his child to Jesus. In this instance, Jesus was up on the mountaintop with his close disciples having the transfiguration experience. His other disciples were down in the valley trying to represent Jesus and, perhaps, themselves. The one who was in charge was away, and those who were the lieutenants had their chance to shine; but they found out that they were not able to do what Jesus had done. There was something missing. They were not able to help this child. The father, nevertheless, was persistent and brought the child to Jesus when he returned.

This particular incident is striking because Daddy was the parent who brought the child. We expect Momma to do that. It is in her job description. When we were sick, it was always Mother who was the nurturing one. I don't know why we don't think of Daddy making chicken soup and bringing it to us in the bed. Daddy's not the one who is going to take aromatic balm and rub it on a child's chest.

This father did something else that we always associate with Mom. This Dad was persistent. He didn't give up. Dad stayed there until Jesus returned. He stayed there until he knew that the one who had the ability to heal his son was back. He decided not to go back home until his son was delivered from the demon. Men don't easily humble themselves before other men. Yet, here was a man who was man enough to ask for help, for pity, and for mercy.

Jesus said to this father, "*Everything is possible for him who believes.*" (*Mark 9:23*). The word "believe" means more than mere faith. The man had a level of faith. That's obvious. But sometimes what we call faith is just desperation. Jesus implies, "Now you must go to another level. If you really believe, then it's possible." Perhaps the father's mind was telling him that it really did not make sense; that it will not work. The disciples verified that by their failure. However, Jesus said, "If you really believe." This message is so important to us today because there's a level of faith beyond our intellect and emotions. When we have absolute faith, healing is possible because Jesus says, "It's possible."

I have such respect for this father because he recognized his weakness, his imperfection and his incompleteness. We need more men who are willing, humble enough, wise enough and caring enough to say to God, "God, I want more! I know that I'm imperfect; I know that I have not been the best father that I could have been. I haven't done everything that I ought to have done as a man, but God, I believe now, and I want more of the faith that I need. I want more of the insight that I need. I want more of that courage that I need to stand up like a man in the face of dangers that are confronting our children. God, I want more because we have to take our children back before the forces of evil take them over. God I want more! It's not that I don't believe; it's not that I don't have faith. Lord, I want more. Help me to overcome my unbelief."

Sometimes this fatherhood business is something we do in the normal, orderly way. We grow up, get married, and have children in that order. It's wonderful when it happens that way, but the truth of the matter is that this is not a perfect world; and we are not perfect people. Many times we get into fatherhood in other ways. Sometimes we become surrogate fathers. It happened to me when my sister ended up pregnant, and her boyfriend decided that he wanted to remain a friend from a distance. They didn't move into a marital relationship. Then my father, brother, and I became father figures. We were there for our niece, nephew, or grandchild. We had to be there. We hadn't asked for this role, but there we were. My brother and I were in our late teens ourselves, but we had to say to God, "We believe; help our unbelief."

This father's story should remind us that God responds to us even in our incompleteness with our imperfections. Jesus said, "Bring the child to me," and he healed the boy. The disciples' male egos were bruised. They waited until they were alone with Jesus and asked, "Why couldn't we?" They could have grasped a clear answer to their question if they had paid closer attention to Jesus' dialogue with the boy's father. The father knew what to do about incomplete faith---be man enough to be humble, to be persistent, to love. The disciples were caught up in their ego-tripping and missed the message that faith would have solved their problem. So, Jesus, the loving master teacher, answered their question in simpler terms. The scripture records: After Jesus had gone indoors, his disciples asked him privately, *"Why couldn't we drive it out?"* *He replied, "This kind can come out only by prayer." (Mark 9:28-29).* My brothers (and sisters), if you want more, begin and end with prayer.   rlg

24. After Thanksgiving

After three months we put out to sea in a ship that had wintered in the island. It was an Alexandrian ship with the figurehead of the twin gods Castor and Pollux. We put in at Syracuse and stayed there three days. From there we set sail and arrived at Rhegium. The next day the south wind came up, and on the following day we reached Puteoli. There we found some brothers who invited us to spend a week with them. And so we came to Rome. The brothers there had heard that we were coming, and they traveled as far as the Forum of Appius and the Three Taverns to meet us. At the sight of these men Paul thanked God and was encouraged. (Acts 28:11-15).

For two whole years Paul stayed there in his own rented house and welcomed all who came to see him. Boldly and without hindrance he preached the kingdom of God and taught about the Lord Jesus Christ. (Acts 28:30-31).

This is one of the well-known "we" passages of the Book of Acts where the author described scenes that he personally witnessed. Paul had been imprisoned, threatened with execution by a military transport guard, and bitten by a poisonous snake. He spent three months shipwrecked on an island of "barbarous" people. No one would have blamed him for feeling a little discouraged. He realized, however, that he had been blessed, because the people on the island were kind and hospitable. He returned the favor by healing their ruler and many other sick people, in the name of Jesus the Messiah. The winter season was almost over after three months on the island. Perhaps there was an early return of spring-like weather. This meant that Paul and his companions could book passage on another ship and travel on to Rome. Some Roman believers heard that they were coming and made their way to meet them. Luke reports that *"The brothers there had heard that*

76

we were coming, and they traveled as far as the Forum of Appius and the Three Taverns to meet us. At the sight of these men Paul thanked God and was encouraged. (Acts 28:15). This gives us the perfect setup for a classic three-point discussion.

Point 1:   Paul thanked God.

Some Christian brothers in Rome heard that Paul was in town and made arrangements to go to see him. When they arrived, Paul's first reaction was to thank God for them. This act of thanksgiving, typical of Paul, sets the model for Christian behavior. Paul was under house arrest, he had just come through very difficult times and he was waiting for an audience with the emperor that could determine his ultimate fate. He did not curse his fate or his circumstances. He did not ask, "Why me?" He simply thanked God when he saw some men who knew the Lord.

Wouldn't it be wonderful to know that people would thank God when you show up on the scene? When you go to the church meeting, do people say "Thank God that you are here?" Or do they whisper words not appropriate for church under their breath? These men were not here to release Paul from captivity. There is no indication that they brought special supplies or treats to ease Paul's discomfort. Yet, Paul thanked God for their presence. Jesus had told his disciples that where even two or three were gathered in his name, that he was present with them. The arrival of these men reminded Paul of the presence of the Lord.

Point 2:   Paul was encouraged.

After thanksgiving, Paul was encouraged. There is something about thanking God that leads to encouragement. When you thank God, you are reminded that God is still on the throne. When you thank God, you acknowledge that God hears your cry for help. When you thank God, you remember the source of your strength and power. Paul was encouraged because he saw that Rome had some brothers who knew the Lord. Even in Rome, the most powerful heathen city of that era, there were godly men and women. When someone speaks a kind word to me about my ministry, my typical response is, "God bless you. That's so encouraging." It is very encouraging just seeing people who honor God by coming to church to join with other brothers and sisters to worship God. A brother once told me that he would no longer be able to serve in a leadership position to which I had appointed him. I remember thinking that we would probably lose him as a member. He will never know how I felt when I saw him sitting in his usual seat in the church sanctuary. I was so encouraged and I thanked God for him.

Point 3: **Paul preached the Gospel boldly.**

After thanksgiving, Paul was encouraged and preached boldly. *"Boldly and without hindrance he preached the kingdom of God and taught about the Lord Jesus Christ."* *(Acts 28:31).* This point does not surprise us. Paul was nothing if not bold. When a crowd wanted to kill him, Paul boldly demanded that he be allowed to preach to them. It seems foolish to me, but to Paul, it was just his usual holy boldness. When a poisonous snake planted its fangs in his hand, Paul shook it off and continued on his way. When Paul landed among heathen people who knew nothing about the Lord, he preached boldly about Jesus the Messiah.

The conclusion of the matter:

Paul was so excited and encouraged because this was not the first time that the presence of faithful men had given testimony to the power of God. Earlier, Paul and Silas had been imprisoned for their faith and harshly mistreated. Paul's reaction must have seemed strange to both the prisoners and their jailers. *"About midnight Paul and Silas were praying and singing hymns to God, and the other prisoners were listening to them."* (Acts 16:25). About midnight, at the darkest hour, these two unusual prisoners were praying and singing hymns of praise to God. The other prisoners were fascinated and mesmerized. They were listening to them give their testimony in prayer and song.

Men singing in the choir remind me of this situation. You may be thinking that most men in the church don't know anything about being imprisoned by the circumstances of life. They don't know a thing about singing at the midnight hour. It's easy for them to sing on Sunday morning, because life for them has been a crystal stair. Not only that, but these men who are singing probably never thought about the fact that "the other prisoners were listening to them." It might be true that they may be just singing to the glory of God, but it is very likely that someone who is imprisoned by life, is sitting in the congregation listening to their song and testimony.

And then it happened. *"Suddenly there was such a violent earthquake that the foundations of the prison were shaken. At once all the prison doors flew open, and everybody's chains came loose."* (Acts16:26). After the singing, the praise and the thanksgiving, the foundations of the dungeon shook and the prisoners were set free. Sometimes God has to shake the foundations of our prisons so that we can be freed to do the work for which God has prepared us.

Sometimes the jailer, the one who guarded us to keep us in our prisons, is changed by his encounter with men and women who are singing the praises of God and testifying about the goodness of God. *"The jailer woke up, and when he saw the prison doors open, he drew his sword and was about to kill himself because he thought the prisoners had escaped. But Paul shouted, 'Don't harm yourself! We are all here!'"* (Acts 16:26-28). The penalty for allowing a prisoner to escape was sure and simple-- death. The soldier pulled his sword so that he could do the honorable thing and end his life.

The physical dungeon shook so that the chains and bars were removed. Why didn't the prisoners escape? They could have easily just walked away. But their spiritual prison was also destroyed. These hardened criminals were so softened and convicted by the witness and testimony of Paul and Silas that they remained in their cells. Paul stopped the suicidal plans of the jailer as he yelled, "We are all here!" We are all here. We stand together.

When some people criticize the church and wonder aloud where the men are, can you make that joyful noise for the men, joining in affirmation with a loud shout? "We are all here singing!" "We are all here ushering!" "We are all here teaching church school!" "We are all here driving the bus so that others can get to church!" "We are all here praying!" "We are all here!" Give thanks to God and take courage. After thanksgiving, be encouraged and witness boldly.

rlg

Church folk

Singing on the Choir

The Janitor

Rock Star Status

Songbirds

25. Singing on the Choir

And now an A and B selection
From the choir
Will satisfy our desire
To hear praises sung
To God who hung
On that cross for you and me
And sealed our eternal destiny
A and B
From the songbirds
Of the Sanctuary Choir
Reflections of the director's desire
To send the praise up
To the very heights of joy
Voices high
Songbird women
Voices low
Men and boys
Songbirds all
Answering the call
To harmonize
Flowing to celestial skies
Depths where God cannot be seen
But can be heard
From the songbirds
Who would have thought the night before
With all the furor and rancor
About church business gone wrong
Even though Pastor says
"All God's chillun got a song"
But there is more mess from the choir
May their souls be blessed

Than all the boards
And auxiliaries
Even the Pastor's Aid Society
Doesn't have notoriety
Like the songbirds
Of the Sanctuary Choir
They gossip and tell all
About the holy sister's fall
From graceful heights
And the preacher's travels late at night
As he ministers to
The downtrodden and the lame
The songbirds say
They know his game
The problems without
Are all solved
The problems within
Get them involved
In places where they don't belong
The director thinks no one can sing
His song
But his next of kin
The piano player
Never could get his wrist
To project straight
Or change that funny walk
To a manly gait
But come Sunday morning
When the pastor comes along
Raising the opening song
A hymn of praise it's called
To notify us all
He's robed and looking fine
Like his old skin

Contains new wine
He marches down the aisle
Behind the choir in single file
Strutting like nothing else
And the songbirds
Climb the steps
To their heavenly perch
The choir loft of Bethel Church
Is filled with sisters and brothers
Finely tuned to join with others
To sing to God's glory
Singing on the choir
Not in, on
To tell redemption's story
In song

rlg

26. The Janitor

Jack had been the church janitor for over twenty years. The more polite term may be custodian or maintenance man, but Jack boldly declared that he was the janitor and proud of it. He kept his private life very private. He sometimes hinted that he may have had a wife at one time, and perhaps a daughter. He let it slip once that a certain young man claimed that he was his son. Jack admitted that it was possible, but he was not sure and did not have a relationship with his supposed son.

He was known as a loyal patron of the bar two blocks away from the church. He stopped in every day after work, drank two beers and then jumped on the bus to Wilkinsburg, where he lived in a third floor walk-up apartment. He didn't have a complete kitchen, only a stove and a small refrigerator against the one full wall in his tiny attic space.

Jack was a dutiful worker who always did a thorough job of cleaning and maintaining. He was a handyman who could stop a running faucet, unstop a clogged toilet and even patch a leaking slate roof. He brought his lunch in a greasy brown bag so that he never had to leave the church premises, until he signed out for the day.

He took special delight in cornering the pastor in his office after asking him a loaded question about religion or morality. He would slip it in between strokes of his broom or as he wiped the mirror in the pastor's bathroom.

"If it is wrong for us to drink, why did God make us so that we like alcohol?"

"Why does being with a woman feel so good, if it is wrong?"

" What you think, Rev.?"

Sometimes he didn't ask a question. He would get a very distant, vacant stare and mention his former wife or estranged daughter and her two young children. He didn't care that his daughter never married and the sons had two different daddies. He longed to see his grandsons and have them to know that he is alive.

One day was different, however. Jack motioned to the pastor for permission to sit down on one of his overstuffed chairs and talk. The pastor pointed toward the chair in obvious agreement.

"I went to see that damn doctor, yesterday," Jack offered tentatively. "I see. Did he have some news?" Rev. asked. Jack lowered his eyes and his voice. "Yeah. He claims it's 'prostrate.' Cancer. And it spread. My girlfriend Carole has been nagging me for months. But I wasn't going to have no man jamming nothing up my butt. Now it's too late." He didn't cry, but the moist, red eyes betrayed the deep fear and stress that Jack felt. As he stood up to leave, Rev. jumped up from his seat and rushed toward him with his right hand extended. He grabbed Jack's hand and pulled him close to him while hugging his shoulder with his left arm. Jack relaxed and yielded to the embrace.

Then he pulled away and stepped back and rolled his eyes toward the ceiling. "There's one more thing. They say I have to go into the hospital right away, and I only have a few weeks left." Jack had never officially joined any church. He wanted to know what would be required for him to join the church, since he wanted to be buried from this church, the only church he had ever really been a part of. Rev. told him that his funeral would be from that church whether he joined or not. He should join if he felt that he now had a saving relationship with Christ. Jack's eyes filled with water as he assured Rev. that he did believe in Jesus. However, he felt that he had done so much wrong in his fifty-five years of life, that he wasn't sure that God would forgive him. "You are forgiven," Rev. assured him. "We will arrange the baptism Wednesday night after next, after the prayer meeting and Bible study."

They operated the next morning just two hours after he checked himself into the hospital. Jack was in critical condition for two days, and then upgraded to intensive care for the next three. Rev. visited him every day and reminded him of their date on the coming Wednesday night. Despite the tubes and wires in and on his body, Jack managed a faint smile and gave the thumbs up sign.

When Wednesday night came, Jack checked himself out of the hospital, despite the objections of his doctor and Rev.'s protests. His girlfriend drove her car to the canopy in front of the hospital, while his son rolled him in his wheel chair to the car and lifted him into the passenger seat. She drove into the back parking lot of the church that was nearest to the ramp and entrance to the chapel. Jack refused the wheelchair and insisted on walking up the three steps to the red chapel door. His son held the door, as Jack allowed Agnes to usher him into the dimly lit room.

The prayer service had begun and they were singing "Nearer My God to Thee" as Jack made his way to the front seat where his daughter and grandsons were waiting. Rev. motioned for him to come to the altar rail and kneel so that he could be baptized. Jack whispered in his ear that he could not kneel comfortably because the catheter was still in and connected to a bag strapped on his leg. Rev. quietly apologized and told him that he could stand. He made some introductory remarks to the congregation about Jack's request for baptism as he removed the cover from the baptismal fount. He prayed a brief prayer, as he dipped his right hand in the fount and intoned, "I baptize you in the name of the Father, the Son and the Holy Spirit." The water ran through his fingers onto Jack's bowed head.

Then Rev. spoke clearly, using his most authoritative voice. "Brother Jack has confessed saving faith in Jesus Christ and has been baptized. He now comes seeking full membership in this fellowship. Is there a motion?" Brother Johnson made the motion that Brother Jack be accepted into full membership into the church and given the right hand of fellowship. Sister Johnson seconded the motion. The congregants came around and hugged their new member warmly as they sang "What a Fellowship." The strained look on Jack's face gave way to a broad smile as his grandsons came up and hugged him. He winced but didn't cry out when one of them grabbed him by his leg and pressed against the covered hospital gear.

Jack died peacefully in the hospice facility two weeks later. He was buried from the church on the following Tuesday morning, as he requested. That night, the officers met for their regular monthly meeting with the pastor. The meeting went very well until one of the officers felt the need to comment on something that was on his heart. "I don't mean to sound callous," he said, "but we know that funerals cost this church a lot of money. We provide the dinner and have to pay extra for security and our custodians. Don't you think we should only do that for our long time members who have been supporting this church, instead of these people who claim to have found Jesus at the last minute?"

The officers' meeting was not the same after that moment. The very dark skinned pastor turned a whiter shade of pale and began to express himself in graphic language that was highly inappropriate for a church. His bald head glistened from rapidly forming sweat. The offending officer looked perplexed and loudly proclaimed his right to express his opinion, even if the others were afraid to stand up to the pastor.

Suddenly, Rev. stopped shouting and became very quiet while his body began to shiver, as if he was very cold. "What's the matter, Rev.?" they asked. He whispered his answer, "When I think about Jesus, sometimes it causes me to tremble." Then he stared at the stained glass dome in the ceiling of the chapel and cried out, "Father, forgive them, for they don't know what they are doing!"

rlg

27. Rock Star Status

Hallelujah!
Turn to your neighbor and tell 'em
Neighbor!
God
Is
Able!

Picture phrases like these
Bigger than life
From more than just a man
From one of heaven's anointed messengers

A Rock Star
Yes
In the flesh

No guitar riffs or
High hats or
Base drums rumbling
Just
Thus Saith the Lord
Cast down to the masses
From this
Bellowing
Thunderous
Voice
The closest thing to the sound of
God
Some have ever heard

Prayers lifted up with the passion

Of a man
Uttering
His last words

Words that
Rise
To resonate off the walls
And
Fall
To a strained whisper

Enthralled parishioners
At the edges of their seats

A Rock Star

No laser light shows
Or back-up dancers
Or pyrotechnics blazing

No

Nothing but the
Everlasting
Sparkling
Promise
Of eternal salvation

Salvation
From the problems
That plague us
From within and without

Salvation

From the
Deepest
Darkest
Corners of the
Tormented hearts of
The most heartless
Among us

Salvation
From the
Seemingly meaningless
Dolorous quest
We call living

Salvation
From the land of the living

Salvation
That moves as fluidly
Off his tongue
As the melody
From the keys
Of a baby grand
Prancing through the land
Of milk and honey
Hand in hand
With lyrical wizardry
Floating through streets paved with gold

A Rock Star

Who is not just pleasing to the ears
But soothing to the soul

Hurry up
And get your ticket
To the show

jsg

28. Songbirds

Sister Mary can blow
And brother Frank can play
And no one may even know
If it wasn't for Sunday

You can see the stress and problems of
Their week
Float away
With a joyful noise
And it's a beautiful thing

A release so forceful
That it brings
Me closer
To peace

They walk down the street everyday
Unassuming
In appearance
And in stature

Those who don't know
May see
Downtrodden and disheveled
Soldiers
Shouldering the burden
But Sister Mary
And Brother Frank
Know
Strength grows
From sparring sessions with

The various
Devils
Of the day

So
Even if you don't know why the caged bird sings
You should know
Why the songbirds play

Sister Mary can blow
And brother Frank can play
And no one may even know
If it wasn't for Sunday

jsg

Chance encounters

Humbug

The Run-in

29. Humbug

When I think
About life
And all its seasons
My fear is to live
Without purpose
And to die
For no reason
On a humbug
Like a teenaged driver
On a Baltimore street
Dead at the hands
Of a lunatic piqued
Who objected to the horn blown
To wake him from his daze
By a driver unknowing
Of the heroin haze
Clouding the mind of the man unseen
When the light turned green
A young life snuffed
Declared to be enough
On a humbug
So I ease through the streets
Of my neighborhood
I never blow my horn
Even if I should
I wait with patience
For the car ahead
To move
Or I pull around instead
Then one day while I was waiting
I heard that sound
Loud and grating
Someone's blowing at me

Like an idiot who must know
That I am not the reason
The traffic's slow
I raise my left hand to signal
With finger raised
Not tandem, single
My irritation must be shown
To the idiot leaning on the horn
Just as the digit
Was being raised high
I saw in the corner of my eye
A figure jump from the car ahead
Moving toward me with bobbing head
And words that made it very clear
That he didn't hear
The car in the rear
But blamed me for the errant horn
Making me the object of his scorn
But that's not all as he drew nearer
I saw the gun by my driver's side mirror
I uttered a loud (expletive deleted)
As my nightmare flashed
Of a scene repeated
A young man dead for no good purpose
No opportunity for human service
I hit the gas and wildly swerved
To roll the car upon the curve
And pulled away at breakneck speed
Knowing that I was paying no heed
To traffic laws or roadside signs
Trying to save my black behind
Again to embrace the ones I love
Not die in the street on a humbug

rlg

30. The Run-In

I hate red lights. So it was just my luck that I was approaching the one on Main Street, at the corner of First, on that fateful day. That particular light always takes forever, but the wait seems even longer when you're as late as I was. It was our third date. I had been late for the first two and swore that I would do better this time, but as the minute hand on my watch inched closer to twelve, I knew I was about to break another promise.

I had yet to master the art of page-turning and driving, so the phone book sprawled out on my passenger seat was only turned to the "E" section. In our last conversation, she went on and on about her love for Gerber Daisies. On my way out the door, I grabbed the phone book, thinking that the extra stop at the florist wouldn't make me too late. I just had to hit all the lights--at least most of them--and I could save time by calling ahead.

I happened to glance in my rear view mirror as my foot touched the brake, and I saw something that immediately caught my attention. There was a young woman, about my age, with a beautiful mocha complexion, driving a sky-blue Volkswagen Beetle. Her huge, frizzy Afro bounced up and down, only hinting at her facial features, as she sang along with her car radio. She wasn't just absent-mindedly mouthing the words to a song, like so many of us do when we drive. She was shouting jubilantly at the top of her lungs. It was as if her entire body had become one with the music.

As I soaked in this woman's joy, my thoughts shifted to my new-found love. I wondered if I could ever say the words that would make her feel like the woman in the car behind me. I wondered whether any of my actions could ever elicit such a response. I knew that I had never been good with relationships, but I vowed that things would be different this time.

I lingered on the thought for as long as I could, but I suddenly realized that I was getting dangerously close to the bumper of the car in front of me. I hit the brakes and screeched to a halt. Then it happened. CRASH! The impact slung my body forward toward the steering wheel. I instinctively shut my eyes. My seatbelt pulled taut around my waist and the shoulder strap dug into my chest. I opened my eyes expecting to see my front bumper sitting in the back seat of the car in front of me, but as I looked up, the light turned green and the car in front of me sped off without so much as a scratch. The scene in my rearview mirror told another story, however.

I was greeted by the powerful sounds of Gloria Gaynor's "I Will Survive," as I got out of my car. It shot out of her speakers like a sound rocket. The young woman, obviously shaken, stood next to her car with her arms folded as she shook her head in disgust and looked down at the mangled wreckage.

"Are you O.K.?" I asked, approaching cautiously.

The young woman looked up at me, and as soon as our eyes met, there was an instant mutual recognition.
"Julia?"

"Humph! Funny meeting you here," she replied.
As I looked down at this familiar face, I noticed that it was attached to a body that was at least fifteen pounds lighter than I remembered it to be.

"You grew your hair out."

"I felt like I needed a new look," she said.

"Well, you look good."

"I know," she quipped.

The awkward silence lasted longer than any red light ever could. Finally, she spoke.

"Dammit! I just got this car a couple weeks ago!"

Although the accident was technically her fault, I couldn't help but feel bad for her. Plus, the pangs of guilt that I had been suppressing all these months, suddenly resurfaced. I was at a loss for words of comfort, so I said the only thing that came to mind.

"Maybe we should call someone. My cell phone is in the car."

"O.K.," she said.

I looked down at our intermingled bumpers and tried to show neither pity nor shame, as I gave her one more glance.

"I'll be right back," I said.

Then I turned toward my car, and before I could take my second step, her words hit me with the weight of a two-ton, sky-blue Volkswagen Beetle.

"That's funny. That's the same thing you told me the last time we spoke."

jsg

Stuff happens

The Proposition

Stink

31. The Proposition

I was glad to go to church on Sunday after a rough week at school. We got a new Sunday School teacher while our regular teacher, Mr. Jones, was recovering from surgery. I never did find out what was wrong with Mr. Jones. He was a tremendous teacher who really loved the students and would bring them special treats on first Sundays. Mr. Julian, the substitute teacher, was a young recent college graduate who had joined the church a few months earlier. He had a mustache and a neatly trimmed beard. His hair was short, and he wore stylish "high water" pants that showed off his colored socks that always matched his Ban-Lon shirt. That was during the week, of course, because on Sunday, he wore a brown suit and tie.

Mr. Julian was very warm and friendly toward the students, especially the boys. I remember walking to the young people's afternoon program one Sunday about 3:45. I had just passed my friend Max's house when I realized that someone was following close behind me. It was Mr. Julian. He began to trot to catch up with me. He spoke, smiling broadly and put his hand on my shoulder as we walked along. It seemed like a friendly gesture, but it made me feel very uncomfortable.

My discomfort increased as he began to talk about his interest in involving me in some strange-sounding activities. I couldn't see his eyes through the dark shades that he wore, but his face showed a flushed glow of eerie excitement. He talked about the special love that he had for boys and how much boys liked to spend time with him in his apartment. My strides became longer and quicker as I rushed the last three blocks to the church. He didn't come in, but chided me as he veered off, about criticizing something that I didn't understand and had not tried.

I had never been so upset or confused. I would wonder for years why Mr. Julian chose to proposition me. How many others did he approach? Maybe there were others, but still, why me? I talked to Max and my brother Jake, who both told me not to worry about it. Jake said that he would protect me. Besides, Jake assured me that he and I could easily beat up Mr. Julian if he dared to try anything funny.

I stayed home from church the next Sunday. Mother and Daddy both wondered why, but didn't make a big issue out of it. I pretended to have a headache. That seemed to be the safest ploy, since anything else might have led to the dreaded castor oil cure-all treatment. I would have to go to church the next Sunday, but I had a one-week reprieve to think up my next excuse. That proved to be unnecessary.

Jake and I were walking home from Duke's house after a long day in the tobacco field. We had just crossed Velusia Street, when we saw a figure coming toward us. The twilight sun and the heat waves rising from the steaming pavement obscured the face of the limping man. Our paths finally crossed as he seemed to move in an uneven slow motion, turning his head away as he passed by. His face was swollen and his upper and lower lips split in asymmetrical, jagged, vertical lines. The dark shades could not hide the puffiness around his eyes. His tall, lean frame was bent, so that his limp was perversely exaggerated. Max told us later that Mr. Julian had invited the wrong father's son to visit his apartment. His bruised face and broken body were the result of that father's wrath.

I remember feeling a strong rush of guilt because I did not have one bit of the Christian compassion that I knew I was supposed to feel. I was twelve, going on thirteen. I couldn't understand why my church would inflict someone like him on a class of young boys, but I knew more than ever what my grandmother meant when she said, "God don't like ugly."

rlg

32. Stink

I don't think I stink
I don't think I smell
At least I can't tell
I know my breath
May not be the best
The Poets wrote during the revolution
That stink was part of the solution
To the Europeanization
Of the nation
I really like collard greens
And a little garlic in the beans
That leaves a pungent residue
That makes turned noses go "pew"
I don't think I stink
I can't tell if I smell
To someone else's nose
Maybe the jams of my toes
Need to be deodorized
By the flower-scented motorized
Plug in's small
Like the pits of my arms
After Saturday night's bath
Which comes after a week
Of work that make most people reek
Of sweat like a skunk
We used to call it funk
When we stunk
Or rank when we stank
Until the poets from the hood
Said black stink is good
It's a smell we should savor

It reminds of our labor
Its fruit sweet or rotten
Self-rewarding
Or ill-begotten
For an erstwhile master
Whose true lasting effect
Was to make me think
I stink

rlg

Swimming in the fountain of youth

Made Right

The Step Show

Man Enough

The Old Man Speaks

33. Made Right

Three cheers for brotherhood
It feels so good this fellowship
When brothers bond
And learn the grip
That means they truly belong
Made right
No new school wrong
Some say it's brutal
Needless gore
Violence should not come before
Knowledge, skill, dependability
They mean much more
It seems to me
Than painful crossings
Of neophytes
To membership in
The dead of night
Sissy weaklings need not apply
They may as well run and hide
Never to come inside
Read in
Escorted without a fight
Never accepted
Not made right
Even lawsuits from another
Cannot deter a made-right brother
From standing blocking the door
Like old school days of ore
Seeking true brotherhood
As the founders all pursued
The gangs understand this well

Putting a new one through hell
To guarantee loyalty
And fearful fidelity
Frats bloody the paddled behind
To guarantee a made up mind
That endures beyond the college years
And overcomes the timid one's fears

rlg

34. The Step Show

I was, in a former life, an administrator and teacher at two major universities in western Pennsylvania. My primary job was to direct a program that provided support services such as tutoring, counseling, and special courses for minority students who were studying engineering, business and science. Most of the students were first generation African American college students. They tried, for the most part, to work hard and adjust to the demands of college life.

One day, one of my staff members suggested that we should meet with some members of one of the fraternities that had begun its spring pledge period. Four of my top students had decided to pledge that fraternity. It was apparent after only three days on line that the pledges were having a difficult time. Their university was very expensive and intensely rigorous academically. Many of the others on their pledge line attended institutions that were not as academically challenging and much less expensive.

Two of the students decided that discretion was the better part of valor and withdrew from the pledge process. Two others, however, were convinced that they were men enough to complete this intense process.

Despite urging from those of us concerned about their academic success, they persisted and they succeeded. They came by the office one day at the end of the term proudly wearing their fraternity paraphernalia. I congratulated them and quickly called them into my office. I pulled out my academic report sheet. My voice was barely above a whisper, "You've been made right. You belong. But you are being dismissed from school." They had each earned four F's and a D for the term. The professor who gave them the D was more than a little irritated when he saw the other grades. These two extremely intelligent young men never completed their degrees from that school, after having accumulated thousands of dollars in student loan debt.

I must confess that I did not join a fraternity as an undergraduate. I was denied an entry in one of the books that recognizes accomplished collegians because I only belonged to two campus organizations. Membership in at least three was required. I mention this so that I can fairly put what follows in perspective.

One of my staff persons in one of the programs that I directed suggested that I ought to do something to make myself known to the students as a real human being. This would permit me to do a better job of serving the students. She suggested, then, that I should say yes to a recent request to be a judge at a step show. Step shows are a part of the black fraternity and sorority systems that allow a whimsical competition among the fraternal groups. Participants show their creativity and dexterity as they step to music, clever lyrics or even tapping canes. I allowed myself to be persuaded and reluctantly agreed to be a judge. My fellow judges were other university professors and administrators.

I remember walking into the large auditorium on the day of the show. The place was packed with enthusiastic students all the way to the last seat in the balcony. I felt a great deal of irritation as I looked at the sea of dark faces grinning, yelling and whistling in anticipation of the contest. These same students refused to come to the free tutoring program for help to learn calculus. Yet they accused the white students who did come of taking over their program. They admitted to studying only a couple of hours a night, but spent countless hours learning their fraternity's step routine. They immediately accused white students of racism for using certain demeaning terms, while they often hurled degrading epithets at the members of rival fraternities or sororities.

Judges were seated on the front row, hemmed in by the long table in front of us and the row of seats filled with hard-breathing students behind. Our judging forms were open to the close scrutiny of these very interested students. My stomach growled in involuntary protest as the step show began. The first group had five brothers moving in time to their crude lyrics, as they stomped their way from one end of the stage to the other.

Two of the steppers were my brilliant ex-students who had been asked to leave by the university dean. The guys with the canes were next. They had the most creative act but they kept dropping the canes. The helpful members of a different fraternity who sat right behind me were careful to point out each drop so that I could deduct the requisite number of points from their score. We gave them the first prize anyway because they were most creative and took risks. This made it necessary for us to slip out of a side door near the front of the auditorium to escape the wrath of the fraternal losers.

Several years later, I joined the graduate chapter of one of these same fraternities. The memory of the step show left me with a degree of uneasiness about this decision. That feeling increased as I found myself having to be involved with advising the undergraduate chapter about preparation for the upcoming Greek Week that included a step show. Our students have the skills, talents and abilities to accomplish anything they set their minds to. When we learn to bring the passion and determination to academic pursuits that we bring to pledging fraternities and sororities, we will change the world.

rlg

35. Man Enough

A man is rough and tough
A man is lean and mean
Jesus meek and lowly
Jesus high and holy
Took manhood to a new level
When he overcame the devil
With only the words from his mind
A man must be first
In fact he must burst
Forth to prove his worth
To the other men
Again and again
A real man can repent
To the One who was sent
To save and reveal
The real deal
A man is not just cold and mean
Or ice and steel
He knows how to lean
And show what he feels
Toward his brother
The ability to touch
And care for another

rlg

36. The Old Man Speaks

I am an old man now
I was a soul man down
When funky was the latest
Cool word
I yelled loud and wrong
So that my song
Could be heard
I marched the streets in '63
And sat where no one
Wanted me
Until my country called to service
I went with reservations
Not unbridled elation
I went to 'Nam
I did not dodge
Though now I need to lodge
A complaint against my nation
As I seek salvation
From the demons who shake up
My psychological makeup
Catfish came back
But he didn't survive
Though he's walking around alive
His mind was buried long ago
back in the delta
where the river flow
Couldn't wash away the blood
Splattered on his brain
Down on the delta plane
He moans at night
Again each day

But the devils won't go away
I am an old man now
Still surviving somehow
Though wounded
And misunderstood
My ailments are not glamorous
My libido less amorous
Than the imaginings of long ago

rlg

Healing time

Evolution

We Don't Give Out Pens
~Lazy
~Hazy
~Crazy

PSA

What Kind of Love is This?

37. Evolution

I've seen it all before
Young dummies trying to be men
Burying their sorrows
And their fears
With their semen
In young vaginas

This song plays on
But the liner notes
Speak of minor hopes
Not achieved

So I roll up my sleeve
And get dirty
Covered in mud
Slung for days
In no place to judge
But far from the ways
I used to be
So the truth should be near
I should see clear
I can see fear
On the faces
Of the next generation
Not far behind
Chasing
The same dreams I had
And still do
I see through
Their macho manifestos
Air from my chest flows

Out
Over my voice box
Rocks fly through the glass house
Of my life

I think twice before reacting
Temporary satisfaction
Won't sustain
So how do
I blend the hemispheres of my brain
And communicate this
So it makes sense

Shifting my vision
To present tense
I
Live for this
I bet
The farm
The car
And
The crib
For this
Love thing

I'm struggling
To remember
That there are better days to come
Deaf
Blind
Lame
And
Dumb
We're all living

118

So thank God
He's forgiving
And He's even forgiven me
For the days when I used to be
A young dummy.

jsg

38. We Don't Give Out Pens

Question: "Can I have a pen and some paper?"
Answer: "We don't give out pens. Is a pencil all-right?"
Answer to Answer: "Sure. Thanks."

I know that I need some help, but I'm not crazy. So how
did I end up here? I guess I can't blame anyone else. I signed
the paper allowing them to admit me to inpatient care. The
assessment counselor in the nice, cushy, front office made it
sound so nice. She was so helpful--made me believe that she
didn't think I was crazy. "I think that the inpatient program
will do you some good. You'll have immediate access to the
doctor. He'll be able to get you right into treatment. If you do
outpatient, it could be a couple of weeks." A couple of weeks
might be too long. I need help now. I know I do...but I'm not
crazy. They know that...right? It's obvious that I'm sane--even
if I am writing this while sitting in the great room of the SRTII
wing of Stressview Alternatives (a.k.a. the nuthouse).

Lazy

I must be lazy	but I can't find the energy
that's what the man said	to bring the synergy
It's easy to explain	that unites my efforts
why he complains	into an outcome beyond
that I am not productive	the sluggish sum
anymore	of all fears that
He wants to show me the door	precedes the tears
and find someone creative	that flow from frustration
willing to do more	that leads to in-animation
and more than nine to five	I can't move
just enough to survive	I have no way to prove
But that's not me now	that I want to work
I trudge on anyhow	so I must be lazy

A few weeks ago I went to the campus clinic. My gray, gloomy thoughts were back again. They get progressively worse, it seems, as time goes on. I'll be trapped in a state of deep despair and depression--sometimes for days at a time. Most of the time I can feign normalcy for long enough to put on my mask and do my happy dance for the rest of the world. Lately, however, I haven't even been successful at doing that. School and work have suffered greatly. The only semi-productive thing that I can do is write. It doesn't matter what I write. When I write, it's the only time I feel safe. It's the only time when the things in my head make sense. It's the only time when I feel like I have control. The doc says she thinks I might have a chemical imbalance. She's the one who recommended that I go to Stressview. I don't know. I'm a bit skeptical; plus, I have a creeping suspicion that doctors are in cahoots with the pharmaceutical companies, so they're always looking for a reason to drug people up. People with chemical imbalances are the perfect people to drug because there are no tests that you can run to see if someone actually has a chemical imbalance. It's all based on the patient's symptoms. If the patient has the right symptoms, give him some drugs. See if that works. If it doesn't work, give him some different drugs. If that doesn't work, just keep drugging him until he quits complaining. Yet, the doc's diagnosis would explain how I've been feeling all of these years. I think I've gotten good at putting on a front. I smile, laugh, joke, and "have fun" with the best of 'em, but it's all just a lie. I go to work and school and social functions and am able, I think, to convince other people that everything is wonderful.

"How are you doing, Jason?"
"Good!"
"How is everything?"
"Fine."
"How's life treating you?"
"Can't complain."

Hazy

It's all so hazy	Is my cry
Muddled,	That may explain why
befuddled,	All is not clear
confused	For me to see
Tied up so tight	Confused and twisted
that I can't lose	Hopelessly
this cloudy picture of gloom	I don't know who stirred
and doom	This chemical mix
A chemical imbalance possibly	That put me in this fix
Obscures my view of reality	It's all so hazy
An imbalance of chemicals	

All lies. Since I was a teenager I've felt this feeling of constant gray. Occasionally there are these little spots of sunshine that peek through. The "bright spots" last for anywhere from a few hours to a few days. During these times I feel like I can conquer the world--which is good because I usually use this time to catch up on all the stuff I've not been doing. I used to tell myself that I procrastinated too much, or that I wasn't good at time management, but it's always been more than that. I realized that I spend a lot of time doing nothing--not goofing off or doing things I'm not supposed to be doing, but literally nothing. I spend hours sitting, staring at the wall, trying to control my thoughts--trying to keep from breaking down. I have to constantly remind myself of the reasons I should keep going. My parents would be sad. My daughter needs a father, but I'm beginning to think that I'm not really much use to them, or anyone else for that matter. I've been trying to hold on to the idea that that's not true, but I'm losing my grip.

There are these two parts to my brain that are in major conflict with one another. There is my emotional side, and there is my rational, thinking side. My emotional side is simple. I feel bad almost all of the time. That part of me only gets worse as time passes. The funny thing is that my thinking, rational self is able to analyze my feelings and conclude that my feelings are often not rational. That's the only thing that allows me to think that I'm not crazy. That's the only thing that keeps me from ending it. The rational side of crazy people shuts down, doesn't it? If I can be rational about things, then I'm not crazy, but if I dare tell people, like the people at Stressview, how I'm feeling, they treat me like I'm crazy. That's the catch 22. For a long time I've kept my feelings to myself--and because I have this fully functioning rational side of my brain, I've always been able to think my way out of doing something drastic. However, my brain has turned into a cruel paradox because trying to balance the two sides is driving me crazy. As a result, the things I hold onto that keep me here are starting to have less and less meaning.

It has all become so bad. Sometimes I don't leave the house for days. I sleep a lot. My apartment is a wreck. It mirrors the inside of my head. I wish I could feel like the person I project to the rest of the world. It's not right for a grown man to cry himself to sleep every night. I know that suicidal thoughts are not normal. I wonder if my friends really care, or if they would change their mind if they really knew me. I don't feel I can talk to my professors or classmates. At best, they would just feel sorry for me. I think it's more likely that they would think I've become lazy and useless; plus, a student that's gone nuts isn't very productive. What use would I be to them? If I talked to my family, I think it would just worry them. They could do without all of that. If I was gone, my parents would be sad, but they certainly don't need me. I'm sure they could eventually move on. My daughter has other people who love her and care about her. This broke, unproductive, underachiever isn't really enhancing her life. I have life insurance. I could try to make it look like an accident.

These are the thoughts I wrestled with in my dark silent place. Those thoughts aren't normal. That's how I knew I needed help, but I'm not crazy.

I waited about three weeks from the time that I talked to the doctor at school before I actually went to Stressview. It's hard to garner respect as a black man. If people were to think that I was a big, crazy black man, they'd go running for the hills like they were being chased by Godzilla. I thought that going to Stressview would be admitting that I was crazy--not just a guy with a problem. I thought that I could, once again, think myself out of my funk. Nevertheless, things just got progressively worse. I was at my wits end. Something told me to just go. I had nothing to lose. If it didn't work out, there was always the alternative. I sat in the Stressview parking lot for two hours before actually going in. It took that long to fully convince myself that I was doing the right thing.

Once they did the assessment and I signed myself in, they took me back to the intake station. The attendant needed to escort another patient back to his room. He wasn't allowed to leave anyone unattended at the intake station, so I had to go with them. When we got back to the other patient's wing I saw people walking around in maroon-colored scrubs that had "SA" stamped across the chest. It looked like an insane asylum. I thought, "These people look crazy. I know I need some help, but I'm not crazy. Do they think I'm crazy? I'm sure they are not going to put me back there with them."

When we got back to the nurse's station I noticed the industrial strength locks on the two doors leading out of the room. The attendant told me to remove my belt and shoe laces and to take everything out of my pockets. It seemed too much like jail. Is this what I had signed up for? The psychiatrist and the intake counselor didn't tell me that inpatient treatment would be like this. The attendant told me that I could only talk to my family members during standard visiting hours and designated phone times. I decided I didn't want to stay. Maybe I had made a mistake. They were cutting me off from the rest of the world. They even took my cell phone. I told the attendant to call the intake counselor and tell him that I wanted to leave, but since I had signed myself in, they told me that I would have to stay until the morning. Only the doctor could clear me to be released, and he didn't get there until 6 a.m. the next day. If I tried to leave, they said they could "Baker Act" me and hold me there against my will for up to 72 hours. At that point I was ready to raise hell, but I still had enough sense to know that raising hell in a mental health facility won't get you out any quicker. So I let them admit me.

Crazy

I must be crazy
That's it pure and simple
My mind is worshipping at the
temple
Of the moon
And the loon
Soon and very soon
They are coming to take me

away
Where I will never see the light
of day
To a place clean and warm
Where I cannot possibly harm
Them or me
I must be crazy

The night was weird. They took me over to the wing where I was staying. It was late. All of the other patients were asleep--or at least in their rooms. The staff members were polite, but they all eyed me suspiciously, as if they were waiting to see if I would snap. As much as I wanted to, I didn't. A petite woman named Frank, short for Franchesca, showed me to my room. There was already another patient asleep on the cot next to the one where I was supposed to be staying. I noticed that there were no windows. There were no light switches in the room either, and the florescent lights glared brighter than daylight. My roommate slept soundly, as if he were at home in his own bed.

I thought, "How can he sleep in this place? He actually looks comfortable." I wondered where his home was, why he was here and if they had tricked him into staying, too. However, my thoughts were not organized enough to focus on others. I quickly returned to examining my own predicament. The staff had given me some bed linen and my own pair of maroon scrubs. I changed into the pants, but I refused to put on the shirt. I felt like if I donned the shirt, I would fit in too much. I would be admitting that I belonged at Stressview. I knew that I didn't. I'm not crazy. I just need some help.

My mind kept racing. I felt like I had to escape, but there was no way out. So I figured I should do the only thing that really helps me to escape. I needed to write. So I went to the nurse's desk and asked one of the staff members a simple question--at least it's simple out in the regular world.

"Can I have a pen and some paper?"

He quickly replied, "We don't give out pens. Is a pencil all-right?"

Here I am, a man with a problem. One who is clear-minded enough to know that I have a problem; sane enough to go and try to get some help; lucid enough to make rational decisions at every step along the way; and everyone treats me like I'm crazy. This is exactly why I feared talking about my problem in the first place; and now, with that one simple phrase, all of my fears have been validated. It makes me wonder. How many others are out there like me? How many of them don't say anything--don't try to get help? What is their end result?

I was released from Stressview the next day after seeing the doctor. It turns out that he didn't think I was crazy enough to stay there. He said I just needed some help. I've always been afraid that people would find out all of the things I've been hiding and decide to write me off, but I've decided not to be afraid anymore and accept being found out as a risk I will just have to take. I fully realize that someone may think that I am crazy after reading this and everything else I've presented in this book. Nevertheless, I have accepted the fact that just like the other patients at Stressview, I am only human; and all humans need help with something. I am just grateful that I have this outlet and an attentive audience. Both are truly gifts from God, and I pray that both will keep me from spending the rest of my life drugged up or in a place where they don't give out pens.

jsg

39. PSA

This is a PSA
For all the brothers today
Who need to stand still
Long enough
To stop acting so tough
And give a little blood away
To measure their PSA
And then the dreaded DRE
Will bring them down to their knees
But chill brother and be at ease
The doctor's interest in your butt
Is purely professional
So shut
Your mouth and bend over
Or pull your knees up
Toward your shoulder
Too many good brothers have died
From shame or macho pride
We need you here on Father's Day
Not six feet down
In cold dark graves
Oh what the hell
I suppose
If he was examining my nose
And not the orifice back there
That makes me so keenly aware
That no man will ever dare
To admit
To less than discomfort
While throwing a fit
Of disgust

While allowing that sometimes
A real man must
Move from suspicion
To trust
"Not up mine!"
He loudly said
Now that mother's son
Is dead

rlg

40. What Kind of Love Is This?

And Jonathan made a covenant with David because he loved him as himself. Jonathan took off the robe he was wearing and gave it to David, along with his tunic, and even his sword, his bow and his belt. (1 Samuel 18:3,4).

I grieve for you, Jonathan my brother; you were very dear to me. Your love for me was wonderful, more wonderful than that of women. (2 Samuel 1:26).

One of them, the disciple whom Jesus loved, was reclining next to him. (John 13:23).

Men do not easily express love toward other men. Some expressions of love by men toward men make modern-day men very uncomfortable. We don't show it, and we certainly don't say it. The fear for most straight men is that someone might think they are gay. The fear for many gay men is that someone might think they are gay. If love is expressed, it must have "man" at the end. That somehow softens the phrase, or at least makes it acceptable. A real man would never say to another man, "I love you." But, he could say, "I love you, man."

David and Jonathan spoke and demonstrated great love for each other. Jonathan did a virtual striptease as he took off his royal outer garments and his sword, his bow, and his belt, and gave them to David to seal the covenant between them. There is no doubt in the minds of many men, that such a profuse expression on the part of Jonathan can only be an indication of homosexual desires. Surely, they think, this kind of "love" is just an intense same-sex lust. It may be blasphemously painful to think of David, the "man after God's own heart" this way. But surely, they believe only the spiritually naive can draw any other conclusion.

David, however, in his passionate eulogy for Jonathan, clearly indicated that their love was neither sexual nor perverse. David loved women in the most intense sexual and romantic way. His love for Jonathan was fuller, deeper, and of a different character than that. He said after Jonathan's death that their love was *"wonderful, more wonderful than that of women."* *(2 Samuel 1:26).* In other words, this love was not the same kind as his sexual love for women. In fact, their love was not sexual at all in the routine, mundane sense. It is more, much more.

Part of the discomfort for those of us who believe in Jesus as our Lord and Savior is the fact that Jesus, like David, was not afraid or ashamed to show love toward other men. The rich young ruler inquired of Jesus, *"What must I do to inherit eternal life?"* *(Mark 10:17).* This question came from a man who already had a pretty good temporal life. He had status in society, wealth, and, we presume, women. Was his quest for life beyond his very comfortable earthly life merely the selfish request of one who had a lot and wanted more? Had he been impressed and moved by the magnificent and miraculous works of Jesus? We can't be sure, but we know that something drove him to Jesus to ask the fateful question. Mark records Jesus' reaction to this wealthy man, *"He looked at him and loved him."* *(Mark 10:19).* What kind of love is this? What caused Mark to describe the deep compassion that Jesus felt for this man as "love?"

Jesus explained to the man that he was so close to the Kingdom. The only thing that he needed to do was to reciprocate. That is, he needed to show that his love for Jesus was as great as Jesus' love for him. He could do this easily by taking the material things that obscure that love, and giving them to the poor. The man was distressed and distraught. He could not do what the disciples did. He could not leave everything and follow Jesus. He was very sad as he went on his way, alone.

Jesus loved the sibling trio Mary, Martha and Lazarus. He wept openly as he expressed his sorrow on the occasion of Lazarus' death and the obvious distress of his sisters. He was not concerned about what other men would think, or about the community's reaction to his unmanly tears and expressions of grief. He truly became one of us and dwelt among us as a man, with the full human range of emotions. He loved Lazarus deeply and was not ashamed to show it.

It is not difficult to explain away the love that Jesus had for the rich young ruler and for Lazarus. One is closely akin to sincere compassion, and the other mimics the love that one has for brothers and sisters. There is no funny business going on here. John, however, presents a different problem. What kind of love is this? First of all, there appears to have been a physical closeness not described in the other relationships. John leaned on Jesus. The mental picture comes perilously close to cuddling and caressing. It's true that each disciple had to invade another's space in order to eat the common meal. However, they seemed to recognize that Jesus' relationship to John was sufficiently different that they called John the disciple whom Jesus "loved." What kind of love is this? After all, Jesus expressed love for all of them and commanded that they love one another as the most important sign that they were his followers.

Some scholars suggest that John may have been much younger than the other disciples, and as such, was regarded as a beloved younger brother by Jesus and the others. They were much more protective and nurturing of him than the other rough and hardened tradesmen and businessmen. This brotherly relationship was so close, that it was to John that Jesus entrusted the future welfare of his mother as he felt his life slipping away on the cross. This is especially striking in light of the fact that Jesus had other brothers and sisters in Joseph's extended household.

I had an occasion to reflect on this man-to-man love in a most unexpected way in recent months. I had been ill with various physical ailments that had caused me for the first time in thirty-five years in the pastorate to miss time from the pulpit and the office. I overcame my reticence and natural shyness to share a little of my struggle with the congregation. This became necessary, because some of the conditions generated pain that could not be hidden from my face, and made it difficult for me to move in my normally spry way.

One of the brothers in the congregation called me at home to inquire about my health and to share the fact that he was facing at least some of the same issues. He had guessed that when I mentioned that the doctors had ordered a biopsy that I might be dealing with the same test for cancer that he would soon endure. He was correct. Since this was his first test, I described in my crude and rude way what he could expect, while ensuring him that the discomfort was great, but the pain was bearable and that he would survive.

He wanted me to know that he was praying for me and that God had placed on his heart the assurance that I would come through this ordeal unscathed and have more opportunities to be a faithful witness and servant of God.

I received a great deal of comfort from his words. However, he said something as he hung up the phone that was very unsettling and unnerving. He was supposed to say "I'll be praying for you" or "You will be in my prayers." My response, "God bless you" had left my mouth before I realized that he had softly said, "I love you." Those words rang in my ears as I instinctively followed through on the motion of hanging up the phone. I wondered if he realized what he had said, or if he had inadvertently ended our conversation with the words reserved for his wife or children. I will never know, because I don't have the nerve to ask him.

I needed to hear, as I awaited the results of the biopsy, that I am loved. This godly man spoke the words that real men only reluctantly speak, even to their wives or lovers. He spoke them to a man, a brother in Christ who needed to hear them at that moment. He even eschewed the formula and did not dilute the impact by adding "man" at the end. He did not say the acceptable, "I love you, man." He said the powerful and risky, "I love you." This is an example of how the Holy Spirit enables godly men and women to speak in tongues and express the love of God in fully understandable ways.

rlg

Fatherhood

Wailing

Out of Step

Who Are You?

Why?

41. Wailing

My baby girl can Waaaaail!
Boy, I tell you
Who knew two-year old lungs
Could pack such a punch

Recently
She's been having fits
Like she's in a knock down drag out
With some invisible foe.

Her mother
Dutiful
Loving
Tries to soothe her
"What's a matter, baby?
You hungry?"
She cries out louder
"...wet diaper?"
That's not it.
"You want your teddy bear?"
Rapid-fire high-pitched squeals

Her mother doesn't seem to understand that
Sometimes you don't
Need
For anything
Sometimes you step back
Assess the situation
And come to the realization that
Life just sucks
I hear that in her cries

I walk toward her slowly
Lift her up
"It's alright."
I say
Trying to hone my fatherly tone
It's still new
Doesn't quite fit me yet

We stroll
She in my arms
Still sobbing
Perplexed that I'm so calm in such a stressful situation

We move into her bedroom
I press play on the CD player my brother bought for her
Sounds of
Thelonius Monk
Wynton Marsalis
Charlie Parker
Float through the air
I hold her tight
Ease into the rocking chair
She nuzzles her cheek between my neck and shoulder
Still sniffling a bit

We chat
"Listen to Bird blow that horn.
Sounds almost as powerful as you did
A moment ago."
I laugh
She lets out a muffled whimper
"I know, sweetie.
The world ain't so nice sometimes.
But don't worry about that.

You let daddy do all the worrying for now.
You just concentrate on being the baby."

She drifts off to sleep
I kiss her forehead
Lay her down in her crib
"Goodnight sweetheart. Daddy loves you."

"Listen to Bird blow that horn.
That reminds me.
Now that the baby's 'sleep,
I've got some wailing of my own to do."

jsg

42. Out of Step

They call you stepson
They must mean
Out of step
Not in step
With me
I'm not your real daddy
I know
But I taught you
How to pee
I taught you
How to stand
Like a man
Not squat on the lid
Like Mama did
Every time you take it
In hand and stand
Remember me
Before you say
I am not your
real daddy
Don't forget
I taught you
How to pee
You think you're a man now
Who can rise up
In my face
A man ready to run
The human race
And that you are
As anyone can see
But before you

Dismiss me
Or claim you won't
Miss me
Don't forget
Big man
I taught you
How to pee

rlg

43. Who Are You?

Some Jews who went around driving out evil spirits tried to invoke the name of the Lord Jesus over those who were demon-possessed. They would say, "In the name of Jesus, whom Paul preaches, I command you to come out." Seven sons of Sceva, a Jewish chief priest, were doing this. One day the evil spirit answered them, "Jesus I know, and I know about Paul, but who are you?" (Acts 19:13-15).

Sceva was the High Priest, a religious man who held an honored post in society. He was a married family man, with at least one wife, seven sons, untold daughters, and the best job in his profession. He had a relationship with God within his limited sense of the divine. Yet, Father Sceva had not lived before his sons in such a way that they could answer clearly who they were.

There are several lessons we can learn from Sceva and his seven exorcist sons. The first lesson is, don't play the games of life by someone else's rules. These sons were probably not very successful. They must have failed in their attempts to drive out evil spirits. If they had not failed, they would not have had to invoke the name of a God who they obviously did not know. They did not say, "In the name of the God who our father Sceva teaches." They betrayed a small degree of honesty by including Paul's name in their cry--"*in the name of Jesus whom Paul preaches, I command you to come out.*" (Acts 19:13). They had to look to the actions of another man, Paul, to find an example of success. They called the name of an apostle who served a God they did not know for themselves. They must have observed Paul many times. Paul had succeeded where they had failed. When Paul invoked the name of Jesus to drive out demons, the demons came out. In fact, the Bible says that God worked many miracles through Paul. These seven sons must have tried to stand the way Paul stood, and say the words that Paul said. They heard Paul use the name of Jesus, but they did not know Jesus for themselves.

The second lesson is that not everyone who knows Jesus is one of the good guys. The demons knew the apostle, and the demons knew Jesus himself. *"Jesus I know, and I know about Paul." (Acts 19:16)*. Demons know who God is, and they also know who the people are who really know God. They tremble at the name of Jesus, but they are not afraid of people who are just playing with religion. You must teach your children who they are. The demons demand to know. If our children are going to challenge the forces of evil, they must be prepared to answer and meet every challenge to their being and personhood. They can't bluff it; they can't fake it. There must be real power to back up the brave words. They must know Jesus for themselves. It won't be enough to say, "In the name of Jesus who Daddy talks about; in the name of Jesus who Mamma prayed to." You must show them the power of God in your life so that they can say, "In the name of Jesus who is the Lord of my life; in the name of Jesus who gives me strength and power."

Fifty years ago, in the segregated southern schools of my youth, a student was chosen once a year to give the speech that called the roll of the distinguished ancestors who demonstrated an ability to answer the devil's question, "Who Are You?" with a loud and certain, "I am somebody." Our children must know who they are, if they are to resist the devil, so that he will flee from them.

The question for each Dad is "Who are you?" Your children learn how to answer this question from you (and Mamma, but this book is about you). Some years ago a young woman came to see me in distress, to seek advice about the doctor's recent confirmation of her pregnancy. She was concerned about how to tell her family, how she would support the child, and other matters related to the coming baby. I asked about her current relationship with the father-to-be. She responded, "He my baby daddy. He cool with it." When the demons ask men who they are, I pray that they can say more than "Baby Daddy." Baby Daddy is selected because he has cute eyes or "good hair" or can run fast and jump high. Baby Daddy is chosen in a moment of irrational lust, masquerading as love, or at least intense infatuation. Baby Daddy is not a father who we can celebrate on Father's Day. Baby Daddy is not in the emergency room when the child gets sick. He is not at the school on the first day of pre-school or kindergarten. Baby Daddy is not paying one dime beyond the court-ordered child support, in the rare instance when Baby Mamma takes him to court.

Dad, your children are asking, "Who are you?" This is the third lesson. If they can understand who you are, they can get a true sense of self. If you are simply Baby Daddy, then your daughter will think that the best she can be is a Baby Mamma. Your son will believe that he should be a Baby Daddy, too, like you.

A recent news report showed two legislators, who were old enough to know better, engaged in a fist fight in front of the cameras in the legislative chamber. The fight was allegedly caused by one man's remark that cast aspersions on the other's parentage. They demonstrated that people have emotional reactions to questions about who they are.

Sceva's sons paid a tremendous price for trying to fool the forces of evil into thinking that they knew God. The demons overpowered all seven of them, gave them a serious beating, and sent them running away, ashamed and defeated. One good thing did come out of their disgrace. Many of those who believed, saw the utter failure of Sceva's sons, came and confessed their sins, and glorified the name of Jesus. Furthermore, some of them who had dabbled in sorcery surrendered all of the tools of sorcery and witchcraft and turned to the worship of the true God. Tell your children that the God of the universe is powerful and able. If they try to serve the gods of this world, they will fail.

Many of our sons have ended up in the juvenile justice system before a judge, and opened their mouth to release macho bravado, that changed a light sentence to hard time. Our daughters, Dad, have allowed their sense of self to sink to a level that made them easy targets for exploitation by someone with selfish and evil designs. The good news, Dad, is that it is not too late. We can atone for a multitude of failures if we start now to claim our rightful place of family leadership by demonstrating that we know Jesus in an intense, personal way. We fathers are ordinary men. But, God can do extraordinary things through Christ who gives us the strength and the power. Be man enough to let your children see you humbly bow in prayer before God. Show them how you confront the demons of life by seeking power on high. Let them hear you call on the name of Jesus who is your personal Savior, not merely an interesting character that you read about in the Bible, or heard the preacher talk about in a sermon. Tell them that they can answer the demons with the words from Roberta Martin's hymn that sustained many in the face of danger, "We Are Our Heavenly Father's Children."

rlg

44. Why?

Daddy, why
Is yours so big
And mine so small?
Son, why
Are you short
And I am tall?
You will grow
If your growth's
Not stunt
You will be
More than the runt
Of the litter
Son, why
be so sad
Or so bitter
Daddy, why
Is my mind
So confused
I'm always puzzled
And bemused
While you seem
So confident
Sure that life
Is heaven sent
While I have strife
And strong torment
Perhaps my fear, Dad
If the truth be told
Is that I'll be you
When I grow old
Maybe it's hope, not fear

Joy, not tears
That the genetic sea
That made you into me
Will be calm and smooth
Filled with your love

rlg

Epilogue

My wife and I have two sons. The younger is twenty-nine years old. The older is thirty-one, the co-author of this book, and the father of our precious granddaughter. Many years ago on Father's Day, I wrote a poem that expressed the panoply of feelings that I felt as I considered my state in life. My boss at work could not disguise his irritation at my way of handling issues in the workplace. My friends sometimes seemed to be more distant and less friendly. The one source of unmitigated support was these two boys who clearly weren't old enough to know better. It is this poem that I first published in *STILL LIFE* that closes this meandering collection of reflections.

Who Are These Boys?

who are these boys?
these sons of mine
they trouble me
with their toys
that multiply and invade my space
the teddy bear and blocks
cars and trains
that find their way to my bed
to stiffen and lump up my mattress
and pillow
who are these boys? these sons of mine
they bother me so at night
with their questions
who, daddy, who?
what, daddy, what?
why, daddy, why?

and they want to hear stories
about goblins, fairies, bears
and such
they listen in wonder and
amazement about things that
never were
and never will be
who are these boys? these sons of mine
they shadow me
everywhere I go
I sneak away to the den
just for a moment of quietness
peaceful reflection, you understand
a moment just to
think, meditate
or read the funny pages
and then I hear them breathing down my neck
nipping at my heels again
who are these boys? these sons of mine
they amaze me so
that they can look at me
with all these moles on my face
and tires around my waist
and extra chins and such
all these flaws that any idiot can see
yet all they see
these sons of mine
as they throw
their grubby little arms around my neck
and squeeze and hug and hold me close
all they see
these sons of mine
is daddy   rlg

Your sons will take the place of your fathers; you will make them princes throughout the land. I will perpetuate your memory through all generations; therefore the nations will praise you for ever and ever. (Psalm 45:16-17).

www.ingramcontent.com/pod-product-compliance
Lightning Source LLC
Chambersburg PA
CBHW060930040426
42445CB00011B/870